D1450978

War, Peace, and God

"In showing how a just-war approach is a living and lively tradition, *War, Peace, and God* makes a splendid contribution to Christians' call to be peacemakers today and tomorrow."

—John R. Stumme—
Former Director for Studies, Church in Society
Evangelical Lutheran Church in America

"Gary Simpson offers a remarkable gift to the church. In clear and engaging prose, he renders a concise account of the just-war tradition. This book is a must-read for all who seek to be faithful Christians *and* wise citizens of a nation currently at war."

—Ann Svennungsen—
President Texas Lutheran University

Other books in the Lutheran Voices series

See www.lutheranvoices.com

War, Peace, and God
Rethinking the Just-War Tradition

Gary M. Simpson

Augsburg Fortress

Minneapolis

WAR, PEACE, AND GOD
Rethinking the Just-War Tradition

Cover Design: Laurie Ingram
Cover Photo: © Punchstock. Used by permission.

Library of Congress Cataloging-in-Publication Data
Simpson, Gary M., 1950-
War, peace, and God : rethinking the just-war tradition / Gary M. Simpson.
    p. cm.
Includes bibliographical references.
ISBN 978-0-8066-5110-1 (alk. paper)
1. War—Religious aspects—Christianity. 2. Just war doctrine. 3. Lutheran Church—Doctrines. I. Title.
BT736.2.S48 2007
261.8'73—dc22
            2007028215

The paper used in this publication meets the minimum requirements of American National Standard for Information Sciences – Permanence of Paper for Printed Library Materials, ANSI Z329.48-1984.

Manufactured in the U.S.A.

Large-quantity purchases or custom editions of this book are available at a discount from the publisher. For more information, contact the sales department at Augsburg Fortress Publishers, 1-800-328-4648, or write to: Sales Director, Augsburg Fortress, Box 1209, Minneapolis, MN 55440-1209.

For Lara, Elena, and Krista, my beloved daughters, that they and their times may enjoy God's earthly peace; and for Diane and Jim Liefeld, dear friends and examples of good conscience

Contents

Acknowledgments

I especially thank David Tiede, past president of Luther Seminary, and Marc Kolden, my former academic dean, both of whom encouraged me to take up the questions of war, peace, and God in our time. I am also grateful for the research opportunities provided by the generous sabbatical program offered by the Board of Directors of Luther Seminary and by a National Endowment for the Humanities Institute grant to study at the Center for the Study of Professional Military Ethics at the United States Naval Academy, Annapolis, Maryland. My profound love and appreciation for Sharon Geiger, my wife, can never be fully expressed in words.

Introduction

In a Time of War

Justice and peace will kiss each other—Psalm 85

We live in a time of war. At the beginning of the twenty-first century the United States of America is at war in two theaters, in Afghanistan since 2001 and in Iraq since 2003. President George W. Bush has declared, "I'm a war president."[1] Three days after the terrorist attacks of September 11, 2001, the National Cathedral in Washington, D.C., held a service of prayer and remembrance, where President Bush addressed the nation:

> Just three days removed from these events, Americans do not yet have the distance of history. But our responsibility to history is already clear: to answer these attacks and rid the world of evil. War has been waged against us by stealth and deceit and murder. This nation is peaceful, but fierce when stirred to anger. The conflict was begun on the timing and terms of others. It will end in a way, and at an hour, of our choosing.[2]

On March 22, 2003, the President again faced the nation to announce and explain "Operation Iraqi Freedom," the invasion of Iraq and the start of that war:

> American and coalition forces have begun a concerted campaign against the regime of Saddam Hussein. In this war, our coalition is broad, more than 40 countries from across the globe. Our cause

is just, the security of the nations we serve and the peace of the
world. And our mission is clear, to disarm Iraq of weapons of mass
destruction, to end Saddam Hussein's support for terrorism, and to
free the Iraqi people.[3]

In both addresses President Bush moved quickly to justify
America's going to war. And whether people in America and around
the world knew it or not, he alluded to something called "just-war
tradition." You find it in phrases like "to answer these attacks"; "war
has been waged against us by stealth and deceit and murder . . .
begun on the timing and terms of others"; and "our cause is just."

People have agreed and disagreed with the president for many
reasons. In these pages we will consider the age-old moral tradition
that he invoked. Past presidents have done the same whether they
have declared war or whether they have refrained. Future presidents
will intone this same tradition. As citizens we have a great stake in
this moral tradition concerning war and peace because decisions
purportedly based upon it are made in our good name, not to mention God's. Indeed, Western civilization in general and most of the
Western Christian churches, including Lutherans, have invested
themselves morally in just-war tradition. It is also ingrained in the
United Nations Charter and in international law. After all, life and
death on a massive scale lie in the balance.

President Bush explained that he authorized the Iraq war for
three reasons: (1) to disarm Iraq of weapons of mass destruction
(WMDs); (2) to end Saddam Hussein's support for terrorism; and
(3) to free the Iraqi people. By now the whole world knows there
were no WMDs, there was no connection with 9/11, as the president
had implied and Vice President Cheney had made explicit, and there
has been no military path to a democratically free Iraq. My prime
purpose here is not to draw direct conclusions about either the war
in Iraq or in Afghanistan. Rather, *War, Peace, and God* has different
purposes. One is to explore the "God questions" and provide an

overview of the ethical framework and development of just-war tradition in order to help Christian communities and persons to assess the wrenching questions of war and peace now and in the future.

Public deliberation about going to war can get morally messy quite easily. For instance, when President Bush invoked just-war reasoning to invade Iraq, in the same breath he also invoked other reasons and sentiments that such moral reasoning finds objectionable. A particularly grievous instance is this: "our responsibility to history is ... [to] rid the world of evil." According to just-war tradition this kind of apocalyptic sentiment and millennial aspiration is not just ridiculously idealistic but blatantly offensive. This example illustrates a significant problem that arises when leaders allude to just-war criteria in order to persuade the public. James Turner Johnson says it well:

> In Western civilization the general term of the tradition that has grown up to justify and limit war is "just war theory." This term, however, is an imprecise one—ambiguous because of the variety of contexts out of which the just war idea has arisen; because of the metamorphosis of the concept of just war over time; because of the existence at any one time of *numerous* theories; because of the imprecision of language, especially in equivalence of terms between different languages; and, not least, because of the expectations of many persons today regarding war, expectations that are transferred to the just war idea.[4]

In one way or another this book will treat each of these ambiguities. But we should never underestimate the potentially devastating effects of the final ambiguity. If people invoke this age-old moral tradition and then in their speech and actions pour in meanings and expectations derived from traditions that wage war for very different reasons, then a kind of blasphemy of the tradition takes place. Now this blasphemy can happen either in an uninformed, unintentional way or it can happen with purpose and stealth, or in some combination. For instance, when someone mixes expectations of empire with what are otherwise just-war tradition expectations, then that person defames the name, the fame, and the character of the just-war moral tradition as it has developed.

In a democracy we are all accountable to one another, to our nation, and to God for war and peace. The 9/11 Commission told us clearly that the terrorist atrocity exposed our lack of imagination and thus our lack of security in the face of terrorism. What it did not uncover, but what many have come to realize, is our deficient moral imagination about war and peace and our deficient political imagination about our nation's posture in the international community.

War, Peace, and God explores God's desire for the strong moral constraint of war and for the wide, rapid outbreak of just peacemaking. It will build moral imagination for just peacemaking. It will strengthen and expand just peacemaking as a characteristic vocation of Lutheran communities and persons and therefore contribute to just peacemaking in the international community. Along the way I will offer selections by people who have thought deeply about war, peace, and God: for example, St. Augustine, Martin Luther, and Hugo Grotius, among others.

Chapter 1 asks why Lutherans care about just-war tradition in light of how God cares about war and peace. Chapter 2 looks at what just-war tradition is, what it says about judging war, and places just-war tradition within a continuum of other traditions on war and peace.

In part two, I show why the just-war tradition came about and how it has developed over time. Chapter 3 looks at the classic footprints of the tradition and how these footprints addressed the God questions. Chapter 4 explores major transformations of just-war tradition, including the scriptural teaching about law and gospel in reference to war and peace as well as why the God questions were formally removed, so to speak, from modern-just war tradition. I also show how just-war tradition gets taken up into contemporary international law and into the United Nations Charter.

In part three, I develop a Lutheran unified theology of earthly peace.[5] Chapter 5 probes why Roman Catholics have reconsidered just-war tradition in light of pacifism's twofold conviction that in principle war is always wrong and in practice just peacemaking is always the Christian default thing to do. Chapter 6 returns to Luther and explores his notion of just peacemaking and his understanding of how political authority is publicly accountable to God for just peacemaking. This strengthens our unified theology of earthly peace, which means that just-war tradition retains moral worth to the extent that we keep it within the richer arc of God's just peacemaking. We will also review ten just-peacemaking practices to stimulate our imagination for a Lutheran "pacific turn," so to speak, as our traditional approaches to the service of peacemaking meet new challenges. This chapter ends with a brief meditation on the phrase, "every church a peace church."

Chapter 7 concludes the book with four contemporary global challenges facing just-war tradition and just peacemaking: (1) conscience-shocking situations crying out for humanitarian intervention and the conflict with national sovereignty; (2) whether "war" is always the right category to deal with global terrorism; (3) the prickly question of whether America ought to be an empire; and (4) the important question of patriotism in a time of war and in an era of global citizenship.

When I consider all this as a churchly person of faith, I can't help but think of God's gift of abundant peace. And when I do, I am drawn to pray. So I invite you to join me in this traditional offertory prayer.

> The Lord be with you.
>   Blessed are you, O Lord our God, maker of all things.
> Through your goodness you have blessed us with these gifts. With

them we offer ourselves to your service and dedicate our lives to the care and redemption of all that your have made, for the sake of him who gave himself for us, Jesus Christ our Lord. Amen.

Part One

The Shape of Just-War Tradition

1

Why Lutherans Care

What has been the Lutheran stake in the just-war tradition? Why do Lutherans care about a two-thousand-year-old tradition about war and peace? We will explore this issue by addressing three questions: (1) the confessional and ecumenical question; (2) the historical and contextual question; and (3) the theological and ethical question.

The confessional and ecumenical question

Lutherans care about just-war tradition in three key ways. First, Lutherans pay careful attention to the strong convictions in Christian tradition, and we like to know what these convictions really mean. In our case this means just-war tradition. Second, to understand what just-war tradition means you have to dive into its arguments about what is beautiful, good, and true. Of course, healthy and respectful argument involves testing out in life and practice what the tradition asserts. This is why Luther so often quotes Paul, "Test everything" (1 Thess. 5:21). Third, the purpose of conversation about how something is or is not true is to reach a fruitful agreement. It is also important to remember that the road to agreement is paved by respectfully coming clean to our clear disagreements.

When I say "Lutherans" here, I do not mean Lutherans simply or even primarily as individuals. Nor do I mean particular Lutheran traditions and ethnic heritages within the broad global household of Lutherans. Nor does it refer to any one or the collective sum of all of these particular ethnic heritages, even though such a global aggregate surely represents a rich treasure that we dare not waste. Rather, I am referring to us as *confessional* Lutherans. That is, we are a vast, otherwise rather different, company of people, not only from diverse places around the globe but also from dissimilar times and eras, who publicly hold in faith and continually test out together in life and practice a set of basic convictions about God, the world, and ourselves. In fact, it is in being confessional that just-war tradition matters for us Lutherans.

Lutherans are very serious about confessing. We favor Jesus' words when he says, "Everyone who confesses me before others, I also will confess before my Father in heaven" (Matt. 10:32, author's translation). Or, as John says, "God abides in those who confess that Jesus is the Son of God, and they abide in God" (1 John 4:15). We certainly favor Paul's missional insight when he proclaims that Jesus went to the cross and was raised in order that "every tongue should confess that Jesus Christ is Lord to the glory of God the Father" (Phil. 2:11). We Lutherans are so partial to confessing that when we offered our first confession as Lutherans to Emperor Charles V at the city of Augsburg, Germany, on June 25, 1530, we placed Psalm 119:46 on the title page: "I will speak thy testimonies before kings and shall not be put to shame."

As confessing Lutherans we are also confessional Christians. And, vice versa: as confessing Christians we are also confessional Lutherans. In other words, *Christians*, not Lutherans, are the original vast, otherwise rather different, company of people, not only from diverse places around the globe but also from dissimilar times and eras, who publicly hold in faith and continually test out together in life and practice a set of basic convictions about God, the world, and themselves.

Lutherans mean something similar when we say we are "ecumenical," meaning of the whole household of faith. In a confessional sense we stress two dimensions of this wholeness, the expanse of space and the extension of time. Regarding the first dimension, the expanse of Lutheran ecumenism includes any kind of Christian and Christian community in all kinds of cultures throughout every kind of society in our world today. We can call this *present-day ecumenism.* Historically, Lutheran Christians have not always been so nimble in this dimension of ecumenism. Too often we have fixated narrowly on a single ethnic heritage, which has blinded us to other confessing Christian heritages. In recent decades we have gotten better in aspiring to expand our present-day ecumenism. The old technical term for this dimension is *synchronic ecumenism*—that is, Christians throughout the whole world living together at the same (*syn*) time (*chronos*).

Take as an example just the Evangelical Lutheran Church in America (ELCA) within global Lutheranism. Each ELCA synod has at least one companion synod of Lutherans in some other part of the world. These companion-synod initiatives are enriching present-day ecumenism for thousands of congregations, synods, and churchwide bodies. When it comes to present-day ecumenism with Christians and churches other than Lutheran, we experience this most fully at the local level, though it has international scope as well.

As regards the second dimension, the extension of ecumenism across time has been a historical confessional Lutheran strength. We can call this *intergenerational ecumenism.* The old technical term for this is *diachronic ecumenism*—that is, how present Christians attend critically and self-critically as well as creatively and constructively to how Christians throughout (*dia*) poignant times (*chronos*) held in faith and tested out together in life and practice their basic convictions about God, the world, and themselves. Now, why is this important for Lutherans and why does this importance make just-war tradition matter to us?

Take an example very different from war and peace. It is well known that Lutherans baptize infants and practice it as a sacrament because it is God's own work to save. Moreover, we persist in this practice in the face of social pressure from significant groups of Christians who insist that people must first make a private choice before being baptized. This reduces baptism to an individual believer's public testimony so that everyone can see that the individual freely and with goodwill has made a commitment to God. Our self-determining American culture reinforces this trend.

Lutherans resist this immense pressure, largely for reasons given and tested in the early church, and then given and tested again during Luther's time, and at other times along the way. Our reasons are based in convictions about God and humans found in Scripture and stated briefly but decisively in the Apostles' Creed. In 1530 at Augsburg, Lutherans officially subscribed to the Apostles' Creed, the first of three "ecumenical creeds" that guide our life and practice. In the *Large Catechism* Luther even notes that God stakes God's own reputation on our baptisms.

As confessional, ecumenical Lutherans we happily continue that subscription. We daily and richly test out whether and how this conviction about God and humans still remains true, good, and beautiful for the world and ourselves, despite great social pressure related to a twofold national arrogance. First, our optimistic U.S. culture assumes that it is automatically better than anything in the past, so we ignore history and practice intentional amnesia. Second, U.S. culture assumes that it is exceptional and that it unilaterally always knows and does best. Too often we practice disrespect toward other cultures and even toward our own future generations. We are congenitally shortsighted and stubbornly refuse to be accountable to anyone else. We forgo repentance. On our good days Lutherans resist these social pressures by being confessional, ecumenical Christians who pray, "Lead us not into temptation." Now come full circle: that ancient biblical word *confession* simply means to "fess up" (*fessio*) together (*con*) about the convictions undergirding our life together and its practices.

The historical and contextual question

Our confessional and ecumenical reasons for caring about this two-thousand-year-old just-war tradition take us to the sixteenth century to find out why we cared at just that time. What circumstances led the original Lutherans to care and thus to include just-war tradition in their confession at the imperial Diet of Augsburg in 1530?

Astonishingly perhaps, it all goes back to that very first officially recorded date of the Reformation, October 31, 1517. On that day Martin Luther posted his *Ninety-Five Theses* on the door of the Castle Church in Wittenberg. Particularly important to our purpose is Thesis 5, in which Luther denies that the pope has any power to take away punishments or judgments other than ones that the pope or his representative has himself imposed.

A few months after posting his theses, Luther wrote extensive explanations of them. He explained Thesis 5 by citing a contemporary case in point. The Turkish army of the Islamic Ottoman Empire was poised for many years to march further into Europe and take it over, which made the Holy Roman emperors as well as the popes deeply anxious. By 1517 Luther was thoroughly convinced that both the Roman Church and the Holy Roman Empire were steeped in corruption and injustice, and that the Church was not at all interested in reforming itself.

Luther read Isaiah 10:5—"Ah, Assyria, the rod of my anger— the club in their hands is my fury"—and knew that in the eighth century B.C.E. this meant that God was using Assyria in order to bring judgment upon Israel for its own injustices against the widows, the orphans, and the sojourners, and thus for its corruption of God's command to care for those most vulnerable. Luther always proclaimed God's living Word in his contemporary context, so he applied the prophetic Word directly to the Holy Roman Empire, which had both corrupted the gospel and oppressed the common people. God's judging hand came in, with, and under the threatening Turkish army. God uses one thief to discipline another. If this is what God was up to, argued Luther, then the pope had no power to remove this judgment on sin simply because a prince, or even the emperor, purchased a very large indulgence—remember that the income from indulgences went into the pope's coffers to build St. Peter's Basilica in Rome. According to Luther's biblical imagination, the only possible response to God's judgment is to repent for public corruption and injustice and to pray for God's own mercy. God's mercy cannot be bought at any price, and only God's mercy can keep divine judgment at bay. Neither the pope nor the emperor were interested in the least.

The pope went on the offensive against Luther, accusing him among other things of being a seditious pacifist who in principle rejects just war. Luther, of course, was nothing of the sort. But the charge stuck and made it into the official Bull of Pope Leo X, *Exsurge Domine* (June 15, 1520), which set in motion Luther's excommunication from the Church. The Bull cites Luther: "To go to war against the Turks is to resist God who punishes our iniquities through them" (no. 34). The chief accusation against Luther reads: "The wild boar from the forest seeks to destroy it ['the vineyard, an image of the triumphant church'] and every wild beast feeds upon it."[1] Luther refuted the charge as follows: "But this does not mean that we are not to fight against the Turk. . . . It means, rather, that we should first mend our ways and cause God to be gracious to us. . . . God does not demand crusades, indulgences, and wars. He wants us to live good lives."[2] In 1521 the newly crowned Emperor Charles

V issued his Edict of Worms, which made Luther an outlaw in the Empire.

Ten years later at the Imperial Diet of Augsburg with Emperor Charles V in attendance, the Lutheran confessors, all lay leaders, again publicly and officially rejected the charge that they or their pastors and teachers were in any way seditious pacifists. Article XVI of the *Augsburg Confession* on political authority and civic life reads:

Concerning civic affairs they [our pastors and theologians] teach that lawful civil ordinances are good works of God and that Christians are permitted to hold civil office, to work in law courts, to decide matters by imperial and other existing laws, to impose just punishments, to wage just war, to serve as soldiers, to make legal contracts, to hold property, to take an oath when required by magistrates, to take a wife, to be given in marriage.

They condemn the Anabaptists who prohibit Christians from assuming such civil responsibilities.

Because the gospel transmits an eternal righteousness of the heart, they also condemn those who locate evangelical perfection not in the fear of God and in faith but in abandoning civil responsibilities. In the meantime the gospel does not undermine government or family but completely requires both their preservation as ordinances of God and the exercise of love in these ordinances. Consequently, Christians owe obedience to their magistrates and laws except when commanded to sin. For then they owe greater obedience to god than to human beings (Acts 5[:29]).[3]

First, regarding the second paragraph, the Augsburg confessors definitively deny here any connection with the pacifist rejection of the sword. Lutherans, therefore, were in no way guilty of sedition, of undermining the military and thus weakening the empire. The term *Anabaptists* is a general term referring to a variety of groups at the time of the Reformation. "Ana-baptist" literally means those who "rebaptize" people who had been baptized as infants but who, having now come of age, decide for themselves to be baptized again as committed adult believers. It is this rebaptizing that united these otherwise dissimilar groups.

In the sixteenth century many of the Anabaptist communities were pacifist. Many also prohibited other forms of participation in civic and political life. In their earliest days some of these communities had looked to Luther for their inspiration. Soon, however, most broke their connection with Luther, and Luther likewise distinguished himself from them. Today, there is a much richer conversation that can happen between Lutherans and our pacifist sisters and brothers than was possible in the sixteenth century.

The theological and ethical questions

Returning to the first paragraph of Article XVI of the *Augsburg Confession,* the Lutheran confessors introduce the God question when they deliberately mention "to wage just war." They make four points. First, they begin the paragraph by alluding to a poignant and then well-known Bible passage in order to make a God point: Romans 13:1-4. Here Paul clearly states that God constitutes political authority with the power to reward good and punish wrong. For this reason, the confessors imagine lawful civil ordinances enacted by legitimate political authority to be "good works of God."

Second, the confessors portray a whole spectrum of civic life ranging from government through civil contracts to economics and finally to marriage and the household, which comprises God's own arenas for godly human activity. We call this Christian vocations and good works. The confessors clearly hold a strong belief in the goodness of God's creation and in God's ongoing creative activity in the world. Just prior to the Diet of Augsburg, Luther had written the following in his *Large Catechism*:

Although much that is good comes to us from human beings, nevertheless, anything received according to his command and ordinance in fact comes from God. Our parents and all authorities—as well as everyone who is a neighbor—have received the command to do us all kinds of good. So we receive our blessings not from them, but from God through them. Creatures are only the hands, channels, and means through which God bestows all blessings.[4]

Third, the confessors list "to wage just war" among the more judicial functions of government, by which judgments are rendered about guilt and innocence and punishments are justly meted out accordingly. In this way a just war stands within the sphere of retributive justice.

Fourth, the confessors purposely list "just war" but they do not explain what it means, much less offer an argument for defending it. They can speak so sparsely because, quite frankly, everyone at the time understood what just war was. Clearly, there are commonly held, basic background assumptions about all these things, which in our day we must revisit.

Two things are important in the third and last paragraph of Article XVI. First, the confessors sum up their basic conviction about the triune God. God works both through creation and the law to produce civic righteousness and through the gospel and the sacraments to produce eternal righteousness. This reaffirms their basic confession that faith alone justifies. Second, the confessors sum up their basic conviction about the Christian life. Christians live out their justifying faith in their everyday vocations where they serve their neighbors' welfare by lives of love and good works. These two basic convictions about God and about Christian discipleship undergird the characteristic Lutheran approach to war and peace in light of God's desires.

In this chapter we have looked at why Lutherans care about

just-war tradition from three perspectives. First, the very character of Lutherans as ecumenically confessional Christians accustoms us to be serious about the basic convictions held throughout church history. Second, the original sixteenth-century Lutherans quite publicly put their very lives on the line in front of the emperor and the entire church by confessing their convictions about just war. Third, those confessors addressed the question of war by actually searching for what God might be up to even in such a grim reality as war. By doing this under great imperial pressure and at great personal risk, those confessors still challenge us today to do no less. We, too, get to raise the God questions in times and trials not of our own choosing with equal freedom. Our remaining chapters will help prepare us for that freedom.

Questions for reflection and discussion

1. What does "being confessional" mean to you? How does it affect how you live out your faith in the world?

2. What examples of present-day ecumenism do you see in your congregation? In your community? What cultural and societal pressures do you note that challenge confessionalism and ecumenism?

3. Read again Article XVI of the Augsburg Confession (p. 21). How might you paraphrase it for our contemporary situation?

2

War Is Always Judged Twice

Moral Criteria for the Just-War Tradition

"War is always judged twice," to use political theorist Michael Walzer's pithy description about the moral approach to war.[1] First, there is judging the justifications for, or justifiability of going *to* war—when waging war is the right thing to do. Second, there is judging the justifications for, or the justice of the means for fighting *in* war—what in war is the right way to wage it. The Latin phrase for the first judgment is *jus ad bellum*—"justice to war"; the Latin for the second is *jus in bello*—"justice in war."

In this chapter, I will first explain why just-war moral reasoning is a *tradition*. Second, I will present the ten moral criteria that just-war tradition uses to judge war twice. Third, I will position just-war tradition within a continuum of three other influential Western traditions about war, peace, and God: the war-realist tradition, the holy war/crusade tradition, and the pacifist tradition.

A moral *tradition* for judging war

People commonly allude to the criteria of just-war tradition, whether they know it or not, whenever they say things like: "Saddam Hussein has used chemical weapons to murder thousands of his own people; now he's stockpiling them to use against Israel, and we should do something to stop him;" or "Before we bomb Baghdad and send our troops into Iraq, we should organize a coalition of nations to set up an economic blockade; that'll get Hussein to change his ways or face a popular revolt." Even when what people say does not match the reality of the situation, they still use standards of judgment derived from just-war tradition. President Bush used a just-war standard when he announced "Operation Iraqi Freedom," saying, "Our cause is just." Even those who disagree with the president, and judge the current U.S. cause to be unjust, still use the tradition's moral criterion of "just cause."

Before listing the ten moral standards, it is important to stress two things. First, just-war tradition cannot simply be reduced to these criteria. Second, it is better to say "just-war *tradition*" rather than the often-said "just-war *theory*." "Theory" might make it seem like these criteria dropped down out of some eternal realm of pure thought, and that our only problem is applying them in a practical way here and now. Our subject matter is more reflective moral tradition than ethical theory, though theoretical considerations play a role.

One description of a tradition helps to make our point: a tradition is a historically extended, socially embodied argument about the common goods that comprise and sustain a community over time and space. Just-war tradition is like that. It has developed over a two-thousand-year period and in many ethnic cultures in various regions. It goes down deeply into Western civilization's intuitive, affective, and cognitive patterns of reflecting on the world as well as into its institutional ways of acting. Just-war tradition (hereafter JWT) ranks among the characteristic genetic markers of Western civilization.

Three further things have been happening over the last century. First, JWT has been spreading incrementally to other global traditions and civilizations. Second, JWT has discovered that some of its own features overlap in important ways with moral features of other civilizations and traditions. Some of these traditions are quite local, others more regional. Third, when features from different civilizations and traditions overlap, mutual learning happens and everyone is enriched.

One thing is for sure: the justifiable-war moral tradition cannot simply be reduced to ethical criteria, as important as they are. Traditions are too full bodied, so to speak; with characteristic communal ways of speaking, feeling, thinking, acting, and relating; with peculiar attitudes, beliefs, loyalties, and habits of the mind and heart. This moral tradition about war represents a comprehensive and integrated way of life, or better, part of a civilization's way of life. But in the twentieth century it went more global because it is enshrined in international law. Life and death, of course, weigh in the balance. Historically, God too has been in the mix—big time!

Ten criteria for judging war twice

While there is no official, single index of criteria for judging war twice, I list ten. The first eight criteria judge *jus ad bellum* and the last two judge *jus in bello*. I begin by naming the criteria and then briefly explain them. I will also identify five complexities when these criteria are brought to bear on a situation.

Waging war is justifiable:

1. when it is in response to the perpetration of a real injury (just cause);
2. when it is declared by legitimate public authority (legitimate authority);
3. when the legitimate authority prosecuting the war has righteous intentions (right intention);
4. when the goal of waging war is to restore a situation of peace (end of peace);
5. when it is undertaken only after exhausting other reasonable means of peaceful settlement (last resort);
6. when the overall damage caused by war will not exceed the original injury suffered (proportionality of ends);
7. when there is a reasonable hope that the purpose for going to war can be successfully accomplished (probability of success);

8. when there is a public declaration of the reasons for waging war (public declaration);

9. when war targets only noncombatants (noncombatant discrimination);

10. when war only uses means proportionate to the value of the target (proportionality of means).

Just cause means that a nation may justifiably go to war only if it is responding to aggression by some other nation or entity. This aggression must be actual and verifiable, and not just possible. The aggressive action also must be of substantial import. That is, it must significantly injure a commonwealth and not merely someone's honor or a small, elite group of persons. Trifles do not justify a war response. The aggressive action must also be intentional and thereby not unintended, inadvertent, or the result of error made in good faith. Finally, the aggression must be unilateral. That is, one nation cannot claim a just cause if beforehand it had provoked the other nation to act aggressively.

The criteria of *legitimate authority* means that vengeance by private citizens does not justify taking up arms against a nation or part of a nation. This excludes piracy and voluntary militias. JWT recognizes exceptions regarding militias, for instance, when the legitimate government no longer exists or is decapitated or decapacitated. JWT has always recognized a variety of legitimate forms of government, like monarchy, aristocracy, democracy, and republic.

The term *right intention* can be perplexing. Sometimes, it covers two senses or combines two sides of intentionality, an objective side and a subjective one. The *objective* sense involves the intention of the overall goal of a political-military action. The old Latin term is *finis operis*—the goal or end (*finis*) of the action (*operis*). Most often, JWT lists this objective intentionality as a discrete criterion, as I do here; I list *finis operis* as "the end of peace."

The Latin term for right intention in the *subjective* sense is *finis operantis*—the motivational goal (*finis*) of the agent (*operantis*) who wages war. JWT prohibits a wide array of motivations and attitudes as justifiable reasons for waging war. Right intention excludes intentions having to do with personal or national character flaws (hatred, malevolence, vengefulness, cruelty, love of violence); political power (enthrallment, dominance, extension, acquisition); economic wealth (gain, booty, slavery, fealty, access, favored status); or cultural fame (prestige, admiration, aggrandizement, meaning, fear, notoriety, legacy, eternal life).

There is only one overall subjective right intention for waging war: the desire to restore a peace that is better than the precipitating situation of aggression. Right intention regularly includes other features of intentionality, like love for the victims of aggression, a willingness to take on risk or sacrifice, regret and repentance for participation in the unavoidable horrors and evils of war, and even a measure of good will to the soldiers who are fighting in an aggressive action.

The standard of just cause means that we judge the actual situation of those injured in light of the aggressor's intentions. With the criterion of right intention we examine the responder's intentions. JWT then expects two things with the criterion of legitimate authority. First, it counts on the wisdom of a political authority to judge the injustice of an aggressive action together with the aggressor's intentionality. Second, it counts on the integrity of political authority to judge the righteousness of its own intentions. These are high burdens because JWT places an inalienable moral obligation upon a legitimate authority to desire peace.

The goal or *end of peace*, therefore, is the overarching moral obligations when waging war and thus the basis for the first three criteria as well as the reason for the next four criteria. It anchors all the criteria for going to war (*jus ad bellum*) and ultimately the two moral standards for the conduct of war (*jus in bello*).

Waging war is justifiable only as a *last resort*. Other means to accomplish the end of peace must be attempted in good faith because of the sheer horror, death, and destructiveness of war. Diplomatic negotiation, mediation, and arbitration are customary means. Cooling-off periods frequently give opportunity to save face and engage in diplomacy. Economic embargoes and other strategies of isolation regularly make the list. Last resort illuminates the bright line that is crossed once war is waged. Of course, there is always more that might be done. This makes last resort the easiest standard to invoke and the hardest for reasonable people to agree on.

Proportionality of ends means that the overall damage caused by waging war must not exceed the original injury suffered. This criterion builds upon the end of peace. The caliber and quality of the peace to be achieved must outweigh both the suffering of the original injuries and the harm that waging war inflicts. This, of course, is difficult to discern, because we are comparing events of the past and present with future possibilities. Past and present injuries are hard enough to calculate but predicting future injury, damage, and political arrangements is obviously more difficult. Events easily spin out of control. Unforeseen factors and unintended consequences are war's second nature. Still, the obligation to judge the overall proportionality of waging war emphasizes the requirement for thoroughgoing critical intelligence and good-faith analysis. Finally, when we maximize good outcomes and minimize damage, we help bring about a sustainable end of peace. Can anything be more important for the future?

Probability for success involves difficulties that are similar to the ones we noted with the proportionality of ends, such as predicting future events and avoiding unintended consequences. Still, this criterion emphasizes that a justifiable war must stay impeccably modest, temperate, and practical. Probability for success guards against utopian or millenarian goals like establishing a golden age where evil is eviscerated and purity always prevails. Probability for success restricts waging war within the bounds of a doable, realistic, and sustainable peace.

Public declaration of the reasons for waging war insures that third-party nation-states have a judicious say in judging the justifiability of war. In this way it introduces public accountability into JWT and places necessary checks on mistaken information, misunderstood circumstances, deception, self-deception, and acting rashly. Most importantly, it helps to ensure that neither war realism nor holy war/crusade expectations are passed off as justifiable-war expectations, as too often happens. This criterion is not always included in lists of just-war criteria. However, it is a particularly important standard in our present global context of intensified international relations.

These first eight criteria make up JWT's bar that must be cleared if we are to wage war justifiably. It is a high bar. Complexities also arise. For instance, we have seen that the criteria, while varied, have a certain coherence about them. Still, do the criteria ever contradict each other in the real world? If so, what then? Do any criteria have priority over others? How completely must each or all of the criteria be met? What happens, for instance, with right intention when faced with mixed motives, which is surely an all-too-human occurrence? What happens when people do not have enough information to assess whether criteria have been met? What happens when those with knowledge about a situation lie, deceive, or are simply mistaken? Who holds whom accountable to the criteria? What happens when one party to a conflict does not follow JWT criteria?

JWT is a prudential moral tradition requiring wisdom to weigh matters of varying densities. People sometimes assert that JWT is absurd because it maintains such a high bar, which can never be met. But JWT criteria are not an algorithm, which pumps out indisputable judgments about particular wars that everyone then will simply find self-evident. Reasonable and fair-minded people will surely disagree about such important matters. Some people might be tempted to throw up their hands, and overemphasize the difficulties or ambiguities of prudential moral reasoning, and insist instead on one or two absolute and inflexible principles to regulate life in the midst of violence. While this posture might help people feel good about themselves, or even pure, it often sacrifices giving real help to other real people suffering real injury from real violence. JWT offers the realism of relative justice, relative well-being, and relative earthly peace.

This *jus ad bellum* description may be summed up in the words of Martin Cook, who notes that JWT steers a middle way between relativism and absolutism: "In all moral matters, as Aristotle pointed out, it is a mark of an educated person not to expect more precision than the matter at hand permits. And in complex moral judgments of matters of international relations, one cannot expect more than thoughtful, well-informed, and good-faith judgments."[2]

Now to JWT's second judgment. The final two criteria provide the moral bar that justifiable conduct *in* war (*jus in bello*) must meet. The first criterion is *noncombatant discrimination* (sometimes called "noncombatant immunity"). JWT prizes discrimination, which we usually abhor as the opposite of equality. But military officers and personnel must always discriminate between combatants and noncombatants when conducting war. Civilians must be immune from being targets of military force.

JWT establishes noncombatant discrimination because military personnel voluntarily place themselves in harm's way and thus accept the sacrifices, injuries, and deaths that they might incur. This is the reasoning behind this criterion, even though everyone knows that a soldier's "voluntarism" is fuzzier and more complex than this. Still, without weapons noncombatants are relatively more vulnerable and thus more innocent, so to speak. Combatants battling combatants is fairer, all other things being relatively equal.

Every war is indescribably messy, truly just plain horrific! Noncombatant civilians get killed. JWT demands on a zero-tolerance basis that noncombatants cannot be military targets or used as military "human shields." Yet civilians still die. Sometimes they are killed unintentionally, by accident due either to technological malfunction or to human error. Sometimes they get killed when an enemy military target is the particular objective. The moral principle of double effect must guide the conduct of war. JWT demands that especially officers but all soldiers in general must choose plans, tactics, and weapons that minimize civilian harm, even when this might place oneself or one's own soldiers at a greater, though reasonable, risk of harm. JWT permits officers and soldiers to take an acceptable calculated risk of injuring or killing civilians if the target is of great strategic value, or if the threat to one's own soldiers is high. It takes integrity, right intention, self-criticism, prudence, and experience to judge what is "acceptable." And it takes a rigorous review process to hold decision makers responsible for judgments about "collateral damage," the unfortunate euphemism for the death of civilians.

JWT's second criterion for the conduct of war is *proportionality of means*. Proportionality of means deals with tactical issues in the midst of battle. This criterion involves highly contextualized judgments. Morality requires choosing weapons that fit the value and difficulty of securing or defeating a particular target, and no more. In other words, don't use a cannon to defeat a slingshot because using weaponry that is out of proportion to the target raises the risk of unnecessarily damaging either enemy combatants or noncombatants. Proportionality of means recognizes the intrinsic moral dignity of even the life of an enemy and is therefore a key component of JWT.

A continuum of traditions concerning war

JWT is not the only tradition in Western civilization that considers questions of war, peace, and God. Three other influential traditions—war realism, holy war/crusade, and pacifism—deserve our review, in order to do two things. First, we must recognize JWT as an alternative tradition to the other three. In fact, compared to war realism and holy war/crusade, JWT is surprisingly countercultural.

Second, this review will clear up the ambiguity, noted in the introduction, that many people today expect war to do things that are inimical to JWT but they nevertheless transfer to JWT these expectations regarding ways of speaking, feeling, thinking, acting, and relating. This slanders, even blasphemes, JWT. Many people then get false impressions about JWT or, even worse, purposefully transfer expectations to JWT in order to promote holy war or war realism or, in a strange way, even pacifism. We want to minimize this abuse of JWT.

With *war realism* a nation uses war as an essential, calculated tool to find meaning and to fulfill its destiny within history. When war is so essential to a nation's aspirations, it becomes core to its self-understanding, identity, and posture in the world. There are both secular and theological versions of war realism and sometimes these are skillfully blended.

With a war-realist mentality people consider world events to be a history of struggle for cultural excellence and superiority. War-realist advocates might use God language or allude to religious themes by talking about a nation's calling or "manifest destiny." Because excellence knows no boundaries, the vocation of cultural excellence tests itself in relation to other cultures and proves itself in a struggle for leadership over other cultures. Each culture must therefore establish itself as a state with power. Internally, state power steps in to discipline people when cultural aberrations arise and when cultural means to discipline people meet high resistance. In war realism a state uses power to extend its cultural excellences beyond its national borders in order to discipline the aberrations of other "primitive" or "barbaric" cultures and thus to "civilize" them. According to war realism this struggle for leadership (cultural hegemony) through state dominance is just the real state of affairs of world history and international relations. War, therefore, is simply to be expected, welcomed, prepared for, and praised as the greatest opportunity (divine providence) to demonstrate leadership for the entire world's well-being. This is simply the real world (God's world). And war is the art of choice adding value, providing meaning, fulfilling one's calling, and deciding destiny. Why do the nations rage (Psalm 2)? Because war realism is the desire of nations!

But this is not JWT! Still, people and leaders regularly transfer war-realist aspirations to JWT. They may do so with knowledge and intention, or without one or the other or both. But truth and integrity demand that we maintain a bright line between JWT and war-realist tradition.

Germany in the nineteenth and twentieth centuries provides an instructive example of war realism pumped up with pseudo-Protestant theology. In 1871 Otto von Bismarck and Kaiser Wilhelm II of Prussia brought about Germanic unification. Already at the dawn of the nineteenth century the Protestant Prussian spirit had provided the soil for this drive to expand leadership for unification. Prussian Protestants were a gifted people and in their gifts acknowledged a God-given vocation. Under Protestant Prussian hegemony, Germany desired to revel in its gifts, parade its high culture, expand its political leadership, and exercise its military might in order to unify the European continent. These theologically loaded war-realist aspirations led to World War I and eventually fueled Hitler's rise to power with the establishment of the Third Reich.

Holy war/crusade is another tradition—actually, various versions have existed—about war, peace, and God. This tradition highlights the religious depth and breadth of war. Believers wage holy war to spread their religious faith. Other things, like holy sites or relics, concretely symbolize the spread of religion. This religious dimension goes well beyond recognizing war as a religious duty, which also may be present in JWT.

Holy war/crusade traditions view all things worldly as exclusively revealed, divinely determined, dualistically defined, and apocalyptically poised for the final judgment. The word *crusade* came from the first eleventh-century Christian holy war to take back Jerusalem from Muslim occupation. When a soldier reached Jerusalem—the journey itself took the lives of most soldiers—the warrior received a cloth cross (*crux*) to stitch on his clothes. This "taking of the cross" retrospectively marked the soldier's entire pilgrimage. These soldiers eventually became known as crusaders and their pilgrimage of holy war became a crusade.

Holy war/crusade enlists true believers who receive exclusive revelation about worldly things. Holy war/crusade traditions do not expect other people to understand their cause; it is divinely revealed and divinely determined. Holy warriors surrender their will and their reason in all matters. They take a solemn oath to obey all orders unquestioningly. The world is dualistically determined for holy war/crusade. Good and evil are clearly and uncompromisingly defined. Ambiguity does not exist: either you are totally good or totally evil. Ambivalence does not exist: you are either for the holy or against it. Holy war/crusade traditions are thoroughly convinced that the world is at the apocalyptic brink of final judgment. God and Satan are at war. Heaven and hell are in the balance. Holy war is total war. Zealotry wins. Purity prevails. The duty to rid the world of evil is the first resort. The evil other retains no guaranteed rights to dignity, religious freedom, physical integrity, or to anything whatsoever. Holy-war zealots themselves seek martyrdom. Reward comes in the afterlife. Probability of success need not be.

Pacifism is the fourth tradition of war, peace, and God in this continuum. At this point it is enough to emphasize that classic pacifism in principle opposes all violence and any war whatsoever. It strenuously protests both war realism and holy war/crusade. It does not countenance JWT because JWT "only" seeks to morally restrain violence and war, even though it does not proliferate them. In part two we will explore pacifism in more depth.

Questions for reflection and discussion

1. Review the list of just-war criteria. Are there any of these criteria that you deem more important than the others? Which criteria do you think are the most difficult to judge in real-life situations?

2. Reflect on the past and current wars in which the United States has been engaged. What should be the United States' response when one or more criteria are not met or fully met? Which wars have met all the criteria?

3. Do you think a war-realism perspective has played into the history and self-image of the United States? How so? What about the holy war/crusade tradition?

Part Two

God, War, and Peace

3

Classical Footsteps of Just-War Tradition

Over two thousand years ago the Roman senator, orator, and philosopher Marcus Tullius Cicero (106–43 B.C.E.) left the first footprint of JWT, though even he acknowledged predecessors like Plato and Aristotle. Bishop Ambrose of Milan (339–397 C.E.) took up Cicero's thoughts and passed them on to his most famous student, Augustine, Bishop of Hippo in North Africa (354–430 C.E.). Augustine introduced just-war reasoning to Western Christendom where it made it into Thomas Aquinas's (1225–1274 C.E.) influential theology, after being incorporated into canon law by Gratian. These are the first big footprints of just-war tradition. We will explore their contributions with special interest in the God questions.

Cicero

Cicero made a brief case for "just war" in *On Duties* (*de Officii*). Cicero remained a loyal Roman citizen to the end, despite his concern with rampant corruption and injustice in the Empire. He rebuked Rome for too often waging war for the unjustifiable reasons of establishing supremacy and gaining glory.

Cicero placed war within the natural law of self-preservation in the face of another's violent aggression. He acknowledged that nature or nature's God had implanted within each species of creature the natural right to repel force by force. Indeed, to defend oneself in order to secure peace is "the only righteous grounds for going to war."[1]

Since peace must be based on justice, Cicero discussed war under the category of justice, the prime moral virtue for community life. Justice is a comprehensive concept with negative and positive aspects. He retained the word *justice* for that negative aspect, meaning to "do no harm." However, he assigned the words *kindness* or *generosity* to the positive or active aspect of justice, meaning to "do good" or to advance the "common good."

Cicero criticized the Empire for waging war without first exhausting discussion as the means to peace. He knew, of course, that waging war for supremacy or glory would not make Rome eager for diplomacy. By giving priority to discussion, he anticipated the criterion of "last resort." He also cited many examples in which conducting war using proportional means contributed to an eventual sustainable peace.

Ambrose

Bishop Ambrose was a bridge figure between Cicero and Augustine. Having read Cicero extensively, Ambrose came to admire him as a "righteous pagan" with moral insight. In recommending him to Augustine, Ambrose passed on two important ideas from Cicero. First, he recognized the priority of justice if peace is to prevail in a community: "The splendor of justice is great. Justice exists for the good of all and helps to create unity and society among us." Second, he made the pursuit of peace based on justice the only justification for waging war: "Courage reflects justice when it protects one's country in time of war or defends the weak and the oppressed." Ambrose based the obligation to defend the weak and oppressed upon his famous insight: "Whoever does not ward off a blow to a fellow man, when he can, is as much at fault as the striker."[2] Ambrose's maxim that failure to protect is the moral equivalent of murder extends the natural-law principle of "do no harm" and remains a core value of JWT.

Ambrose made two more original contributions to JWT. First, he recognized justice as the core of what God desires for human community and therefore placed it firmly at the forefront of the Christian faith. In this way he specifically introduced the God question into JWT, giving it a theological basis: "Those who love justice must first direct it to God; second, to their country; third, to parents; and last, to all people. This is the way in which nature reflects it." Second, Ambrose introduced the distinction between law and gospel into Christian reflection on justified war: "The law calls for reciprocal vengeance; the Gospel commands us to return love for hostility, good will for hatred, prayers for curses"; "Indeed, even if someone comes up against an armed thief, he cannot return blow for blow lest in the act of protecting himself he weaken the virtue of love. The Gospel supports this position in a clear and obvious way: 'Put up your sword; everyone who kills with the sword will be killed by it' (Matthew 26:52)."[3] Ambrose's thinking took root in Augustine.

Augustine

Augustine is the most important figure in the historical development of JWT from the perspective of the Christian faith. He made five contributions. First, he learned the basic insights of just-war reasoning and the relevant God questions from Ambrose. While he defended all of the first four criteria, he is particularly famous for what he said about the "end of peace."

Peace should be the object of your desire; war should be waged only as a necessity, and waged only that God may by it deliver men from the necessity and preserve them in peace. For peace is not sought in order to the kindling of war, but war is waged in order that peace may be obtained. Therefore, even in waging war, cherish the spirit of a peacemaker, that, by conquering those whom you attack, you may lead them back to the advantages of peace; . . . Let necessity, therefore, and not your will, slay the enemy who fights against you.[4]

Augustine rejected wars of self-interested desire because God would bless only wars of justified necessity with lasting peace based in justice. "For it is the wrongdoing of the opposing party which compels the wise man to wage just wars." This "just cause" distinction between wars of desire and wars of necessity became JWT's soul.[5]

Second, Augustine incorporated JWT within a theological understanding of politics. In his influential *City of God* he asked what the purpose of worldly politics is. When the Goths sacked Rome in 410, the pagans of Rome blamed Christianity. Christian emperors had ruled the Roman Empire for nearly a century and had abandoned the pagan gods whom the pagans claimed had kept the Empire strong. Now the Empire was paying the price for becoming Christian.

Augustine defended Christianity against this charge by sharply distinguishing the city of God from the human earthly city of history and politics. Two different "loves" rule these two separate cities. Love of God rules the city of God; love of self rules the earthly city. Christians and the church live here on earth as resident aliens in a pilgrim condition since our true home is in heaven. Yet as Augustine noted, "the peace which we enjoy in this life, . . . is rather the solace of our misery than the positive enjoyment of felicity."[6] Indeed, Augustine had a sober, even somber, view about the level of joy that any temporal city could provide, and this included family life as well. When it comes to war, no one, especially Christians, should wage it in order to create a version of the city of God here on earth. We can attain only a mere modicum of peace based upon a small measure of justice. Even a necessary war is limited in what it can accomplish. Still, God provides that small measure of justice by instituting government, which bears the sword with a mournful duty.

By placing just war within a larger theological framework, Augustine did something very important. He was not, however, the first to allow Christians to be soldiers under just-war-like conditions. For at least 150 years prior to Constantine, rudimentary just-war reasoning was common among Christians. Augustine, Aquinas, Luther, and Calvin all cite New Testament examples of soldiers who trusted and followed Jesus and no one required them to quit being soldiers. There is evidence of Christian soldiers in the early church, although there were not many because most early Christians did not come from the soldiering class of Roman citizenship.[7] This counters the standard but wrong account among both pacifist Christians and many within JWT churches that Jesus was a pacifist and so was the church of the first three centuries. In this misleading account only after Constantine became emperor early in the fourth century and Augustine came along a hundred years later were Christians morally allowed to be soldiers.

Third, Augustine carefully used common distinctions in order to interpret certain Scripture texts without abandoning just-war reasoning, which is supported by other Scripture texts. For instance, he made a distinction between the self-defense of Christians as private citizens and Christians as public officials defending others or the nation.

> As to killing others in order to defend one's own life, I do not approve of this, unless one happens to be a soldier or public functionary acting, not for himself, but in defense of others or of the

city in which he resides, if he act according to the commission lawfully given him, and in the manner becoming his office. When, however, men are prevented, by being alarmed, from doing wrong, it may be said that a real service is done to themselves. The precept, "Resist not evil" [Matthew 5:39], was given to prevent us from taking pleasure in revenge, in which the mind is gratified by the sufferings of others, but not to make us neglect the duty of restraining men from sin.[8]

Even when Christians must kill in a justifiable war, Augustine admonishes them that they are required by Jesus to do so with a peace-loving heart.

Fourth, Augustine rooted its moral reasoning in love. Starting from the two love commands—love the Lord your God with all your heart, and with all your soul, and with all your mind; and your neighbor as yourself—he held that love is the basis of all morality. He knew how counterintuitive connecting love with war's violence would seem. He wrote a letter to his friend Marcellinus, a Roman ruler in Carthage, in which he dealt at length with Jesus' Sermon on the Mount and compared a just war with a father who in love punishes a son who persists in wrong.

These precepts concerning patience ought to be always retained in the habitual discipline of the heart, and the benevolence, which prevents the recompensing of evil for evil, must be always fully cherished in the disposition. At the same time, many things must be done in correcting with a certain benevolent severity.... For in the correction of a son, even with some sternness, there is assuredly no diminution of a father's love; yet, in the correction, that is done which is received with reluctance and pain by one whom it seems necessary to heal by pain.[9]

Augustine's fifth "contribution" to JWT for centuries sowed immeasurable mayhem throughout the world and inflicted enormous damage on the moral tradition of justifiable war (thus the quotation marks). He also "contributed" the DNA for holy war/crusade.

The context for this "contribution" started a century before Augustine, when Constantine became the first Christian Roman emperor. The status of Christianity began to shift. First, in 312 C.E. Constantine fought a rival for the throne at the Battle of the Milvian Bridge. The following year he issued the Edict of Milan, which declared that the Empire would no longer persecute or discriminate against the Christian faith but would tolerate it. Finally, he convened the imperial Council of Nicaea (325 C.E.), which unified Christianity internally and gave it added legitimacy in the Empire. The Council did not, however, make other religions illegal. It was Theodosius, a Christian, who established Christianity as the Empire's only religion and through a series of decrees made other religions illegal after becoming emperor in 380 C.E.

Within this context Augustine set out his argument in a letter to the ruler Boniface, who had to deal with the Donatist controversy. Donatists were Christians who were extremely serious about moral purity and at times violently persecuted other Christians who were not so serious. Augustine advised Boniface to use his political office to discipline or, if need be, eliminate the Donatist heretics, by this reasoning. In this letter, Augustine combines his analogy of paternal love regarding punishment with Paul's statement in Romans, "there is no authority except from God, . . . For rulers are not a terror to good conduct but to bad. . . . for the authority does not bear the sword in vain! It is the servant of God to execute wrath on the wrongdoer" (Rom. 13:1-4). So far Augustine has made no innovation in just-war reasoning.

Next, Augustine rhetorically asks Boniface, "How then are kings to serve the Lord with fear, except by preventing and chastising with religious severity all those acts which are done in opposition to the commandments of the Lord?" Here Augustine asserts that political authority bears the sword in order to enforce not just the neighbor-love commandments of the second table of the Decalogue, but also the love-God commandments of the first table. "For why," asks Augustine, "when free-will is given by God to man, should adulteries be punished by the laws, and sacrilege allowed? Is it a lighter matter that a soul should not keep faith with God, than that a woman should be faithless to her husband?" His reasoning here has had dire consequences for JWT!

Augustine guards a potential weakness in his train of thought by stating: "It is indeed better (as no one ever could deny) that men should be led to worship God by teaching, than that they should be driven to it by fear of punishment or pain; but it does not follow that because the former course produces the better men, therefore those who do not yield to it should be neglected." And he "strengthens" his flank by adding: "For many have found advantage (as we have proved, and are daily proving by actual experiment), in being first compelled by fear or pain, so that they might afterwards be influenced by teaching, or might follow out in act what they had already learned in word." Then he adds what he took to be the *coup de grace*, "But while those are better who are guided aright by love, those are certainly more numerous who are corrected by fear."[10]

This "contribution" fueled centuries of imperial Christendom and the fateful history of the crusades and holy wars. While Augustine had at times sharply distinguished the city of God from the earthly city, here he fused them dangerously. No one seriously challenged his holy war/crusade reasoning until the Reformation era. Over the next seven centuries, Augustine's just-war reasoning took root throughout the Holy Roman Empire and officially became canon law when Johannes Gratian included it in *The Concord of Discordant Canons*, also called the *Decretum*, of the twelfth century. With this, Augustine's theological judgments became not simply part of church rule but enforceable imperial law.

Aquinas

After his death in 1274, Thomas Aquinas became known as "the angelic doctor." This title signifies his unsurpassable status in the Roman Catholic Church even today. As the epitome of a university theologian, Aquinas gave JWT its scholarly status. In his greatest work, *Summa Theologica* ("The Summation of Theology"), he took Augustine's thinking and worked it into a brief, ordered, and authoritative text for students in the university. Aquinas considered war under two topics: first under charity, whose principle action is to love; and second under religious orders.

Aquinas regarded charity, along with faith and hope, to be the supernatural virtues bestowed by grace. These three supernatural virtues bring the four natural virtues—prudence, justice, fortitude, and temperance—to perfection. After he defined charity and identified its basic actions, he dealt with the vices that oppose charity, including war.

Aquinas begins his examination of war, as he begins every topic in the *Summa*, by posing a question: "Is it always sinful to wage war?" Notice that he presumes war's sinfulness! Any other judgment regarding war would have to meet rigorous criteria. Then he continues the dialogical pattern he uses throughout the *Summa*. He first raises objections to the question, often quoting Scripture, the church fathers, philosophers, poets, and other writers. In his first objection he quotes Jesus, "All that take the sword shall perish with the sword" (Matt. 26:52), and concludes, "Therefore all wars are unlawful." In his second objection he again quotes Jesus, "But I say to you not to resist" (Matt. 5:39) and then quotes Paul, "Not revenging yourselves, my dearly beloved, but give place unto wrath" (Rom. 12:19). He concludes, "Therefore war is always sinful."[11]

Next, as is his pattern, Aquinas quotes some respected authority with a contrary opinion to the objections. Not surprisingly, he quotes Augustine, using this passage:

If the Christian Religion forbade war altogether, those who sought salutary advice in the Gospel would rather have been counseled to cast aside their arms, and to give up soldiering altogether. On the contrary, they were told: "Do violence to no one . . . and be content with your pay" [Luke 3:14]. If he commanded them to be content with their pay, he did not forbid soldiering.

Finally, Aquinas gives his own reply to the original question and follows up this reply with his own reply to each of the original objections. Here is his reply to the original question.

I answer that, In order for a war to be just, three things are necessary. First, the authority of the sovereign by whose command the war is to be waged. . . .

Secondly, a just cause is required, namely that those who are attacked, should be attacked because they deserve it on account of some fault. . . .

Thirdly, it is necessary that the belligerents should have a rightful intention, so that they intend the advancement of good, or the avoidance of evil. . . .

He quotes Scripture twice (Rom. 13:4 and Ps. 82:4) to support the legitimate authority criterion. He also cites Augustine, and only Augustine, at least once for each criterion, as well as to support three of his four replies to the objections.

Once Aquinas enumerated these three necessary things, he set the first three criteria in stone and handed them on as we have them today. He also put sovereign authority first because the biggest concern in medieval times was the proliferation of war instigated by wealthy private individuals against other individuals or local political jurisdictions.

As stated earlier, Aquinas thought about war also under the topic of the religious orders of the Catholic Church. First, he establishes what a religious order is and does. Then he asks a particular question: "[Can] a religious order . . . be directed to soldiering?"[12] He notes that religious orders are to serve God and help the neighbor. Soldiers also serve "the defense of divine worship and public safety, or also of the poor and oppressed" when they do so under legitimate authority with just cause and right intention. He concludes, "Hence a religious order may be fittingly established for soldiering."

Aquinas retrieved Augustine's fifth "contribution" and expanded it to include the church. First, legitimate temporal authority can use the sword to enforce both the second table of the Ten Commandments in order to maintain public safety and the first table in order to maintain right worship. Second, the church under the pope and bishops can bear the sword through the soldiering of religious orders, something even Augustine had not contemplated. Third, the book of First Maccabees provides the biblical framework (medieval Christianity considered Maccabees to be Old Testament Scripture). Finally, Aquinas asserts the legitimacy of the Crusades and thereby the "Christian" holy-war tradition. Since 1095 c.e. popes and bishops had made crusading a religious satisfaction for doing wrong. Aquinas states: "soldiering which is directed to the service of God is imposed as a penance on some people, as in the case of those upon whom it is enjoined to take arms in defense of the Holy Land."

Aquinas left a split legacy. On the one hand, he clarified and consolidated key JWT criteria. On the other hand, he passed along Augustine's holy-war reasoning and even expanded it by legitimizing crusade as Christian penance. This fed the problem of alien expectations being transferred into JWT. Three hundred years will pass before Christian theologians again take up war and peace questions. Because of the very different circumstances in both the church and the world, they will critically transform the tradition, beginning with a rejection of holy war/crusade.

Questions for reflection and discussion

1. How does Cicero's concept of the negative and positive aspects of justice continue to manifest itself in contemporary society? Have justice and peace been divorced from one another? How?
2. What does it mean to "cherish the spirit of a peacemaker"?
3. Do you see any ways in which modern wars seem to violate Augustine's caution against waging war to create a version of the city of God here on earth? How has Augustine's fifth "contribution" abetted such violations?
4. Do you believe Christians should serve as soldiers? Why or why not?

4

Transforming Footsteps of Just-War Tradition

The basic footsteps of JWT were in place by Martin Luther's time (1483–1546). But Luther and his contemporary Francisco de Vitoria (1483–1546), Catholic theologian at the University of Salamanca, Spain, began to transform the tradition in important ways. Then a century later came the Dutch jurist Hugo Grotius (1583–1645), who transformed JWT more than anyone, including how to treat the God questions. He prepared it for the modern world, which carried it into the era of International Humanitarian Law (1863 to the present) and the United Nations (founded in 1945).

Luther

Martin Luther made six contributions to JWT. First, he intentionally brought just-war reasoning into the sixteenth-century reform of the church. He considered JWT's basic tenets to be right because they conform to the distinction between law and gospel. In *Whether Soldiers Too Can Be Saved* he used Augustine's critical distinction between necessity and desire:

> No war is just, even if it is a war between equals, unless one has such a good reason for fighting and such a good conscience that he can say, "My neighbor compels and forces me to fight, though I would rather avoid it." In that case, it can be called not only war, but lawful self-defense, for we must distinguish between wars that

someone begins because that is what he wants to do and does before anyone else attacks him, and those wars that are provoked when an attack is made by someone else. The first kind can be called wars of desire; the second, wars of necessity. The first kind is of the devil; God does not give good fortune to the man who wages that kind of war. The second kind are human disasters; God help in them![1]

Second, Luther used the biblical distinction between law and gospel to interpret the classic biblical passages that address violence and the sword. He was aware that pacifists approach these same passages in a very different way. In 1523 he received a request from John the Steadfast, who would soon become his own prince. John wanted to know whether he would be able to exercise the full range of powers of the princely office with a good Christian conscience now that he had become an ardent defender of the gospel and the Reformation cause. He was concerned specifically about the coercive and violent power of "the sword," which belonged to political authority according to a set of biblical passages, most prominently Romans 13:1-4 and 1 Peter 2:13-14.

Some pacifist Anabaptists were confronting John with another set of biblical passages like those from Jesus' Sermon on the Mount, "do not resist an evildoer" and "turn the other cheek"; from Romans, "never avenge yourselves . . . vengeance is mine, I will repay, says the Lord"; and from 1 Peter, "do not repay evil for evil." The pacifists said that these passages mean that no true Christian, including a Christian prince, could ever use "the sword" under any circumstance, either in a criminal court proceeding or to keep domestic peace or, analogously, to wage any kind of war.

Luther sent a now-famous answer to John, *Temporal Authority: To What Extent It Should Be Obeyed*. Before he answered the pacifist interpretation, he had to reply to the standard medieval interpretation of these same passages that the pacifists were using. In medieval

Catholicism, a prince could bear the sword and remain a Christian in good conscience because these turn-the-other-cheek passages were special "counsels" spoken only to those who dedicated themselves to "Christian perfection"—those who took priestly or monastic vows. Luther rejected this kind of interpretation of Scripture as "wantonness and caprice." Rather, these passages "apply to everyone alike." He rejected all class distinctions between perfect and ordinary Christians based on status markers like "outwardly male or female, prince or peasant, monk or layman."[2]

In order to reply to the pacifist interpretation Luther instructed John on the basic distinction between law and gospel. In the law God commands sinners what to do and not do and compels us to follow these commands. In the gospel God promises and proclaims what God has done for sinners and creates faith and love. The law therefore restrains sin and evil, protects the vulnerable and all of us in our vulnerabilities, and promotes civil goodness and justice. The law *curbs* sin and evil; it cannot *cure* sin or rid the world of evil. Only the gospel can heal sinners now through forgiveness and on the last day permanently finish off all sin and evil.

The law therefore preserves this world where sin and evil still prowl around like "wolves, lions, [and] eagles." Luther was very realistic about all this. In *Temporal Authority* he calls the law's work of preservation "the kingdom of the world"; elsewhere he calls it "God's left-hand rule." The gospel, on the other hand, inaugurates in this world "the kingdom of God" or "God's right-hand rule" of the world. God's right-hand rule comes into the world right now by the work of the Holy Spirit through Word and Sacrament in the church. God's right-hand rule will come fully as the New Jerusalem on the last day. Then sin, death, the devil, and even God's own law will come to a cosmic end. By faith alone their reigning dominance already comes to an end for the Christian church.

In summary, God institutes two modes of governing the world, each with its own integrity, purpose, and power: "the spiritual, by which the Holy Spirit produces Christians and righteous people under Christ; and the temporal, which restrains the un-Christian and wicked so that—no thanks to them—they are obliged to keep still and to maintain an outward peace." Christians must "carefully distinguish between these two governments. Both must be permitted to remain: the one to produce righteousness, the other to bring about external peace and prevent evil deeds. Neither one is sufficient in the world without the other."[3]

Luther told John that he would live according to these passages only by caring for the distinction between law and gospel and the "two [or both] kingdoms." No Christian will resort to the law and "the sword" of temporal political authority in two kinds of circumstances: "among themselves" as the church and "by and for themselves" in any circumstance.[4] In the first circumstance John honors the difference between the church and the world; in the second he honors the difference between acting in one's own self-interest and acting in the interest of the neighbor.

Luther learned the biblical distinction between self and neighbor from Ambrose and Augustine and passed it along to John:

> Since a true Christian lives and labors on earth not for himself alone but for his neighbor, he does by the very nature of his spirit even what he himself has no need of, but is needful and useful to his neighbor. Because the sword is most beneficial and necessary for the whole world in order to preserve peace, punish sin, and restrain the wicked, the Christian submits most willingly to the rule of the sword, pays his taxes, honors those in authority, serves, helps, and does all he can to assist governing authority, that it may continue to function and be held in honor and fear. Although he has no need of these things for himself—to him they are not essential—nevertheless, he concerns himself about what is serviceable and of benefit to others, as Paul teaches in Ephesians 5.[5]

In making these three sets of distinctions Luther brought the two sets of biblical passages "into harmony," and provided the harmony of the Christian witness of faith and life. John can exercise his vocation in the office of prince according to a twofold mandate from God: on the one hand, to represent God by implementing God's just law and, on the other hand, to serve the vulnerable neighbor rather than the self.

Like Augustine, Luther considered the sword to be a work of love whose only legitimate purpose is to preserve temporal peace:

> Now slaying and robbing do not seem to be works of love. A simple man therefore does not think it is a Christian thing to do. In truth, however, even this is a work of love.... [W]hen I think of a soldier fulfilling his office by punishing the wicked, killing the wicked, and creating so much misery, it seems an un-Christian work completely contrary to Christian love. But when I think of how it protects the good and keeps and preserves wife and child, house and farm, property, and honor and peace, then I see how precious and godly this work is; and I observe that it amputates a leg or a hand, so that the whole body may not perish....
>
> What men write about war, saying that it is a great plague, is all true. But they should also consider how great the plague is that [just] war prevents.[6]

Third, Luther criticized severely his famous teacher Augustine, along with anyone who followed in Augustine's theocratic and holy war/crusade footsteps. He makes this criticism in the second part of *Temporal Authority*, where he establishes the limits of political authority, which also establishes the right use of the sword. This is what Luther's subtitle means, *To What Extent It Should Be Obeyed.*

Does God give political authority the competencies and therefore the right and obligation to use the sword in order to bring anyone to eternal life, salvation, and faith? Absolutely not! Under no circumstance should political authority "coerce the people with their laws and commandments into believing this or that." God gives "no power over souls" to the office of prince or any other political office. Luther cited Matthew 16:18 and John 10:27 and concluded, "In matters which concern the salvation of souls nothing but God's Word shall be taught and accepted. . . . Therefore, it is futile and impossible to command or compel anyone by force to believe this or that. The matter must be approached in a different way. Force will not accomplish it." Force and violence are even counterproductive. "For faith is a free act, to which no one can be forced. Indeed, it is a work of God in the spirit, not something which outward authority should compel or create." He then cited "the common saying," which even Augustine had on one occasion cited, "No one can or ought to be forced to believe." Coercion could only create hypocrites, not real faith.[7]

God institutes political authority and the sword only for the "outward compliance of the mouth and the hand," the second table of the Ten Commandments. Luther opposed the theocratic tendencies in both Augustine and Aquinas. He specifically tested the theocracy question by asking whether God institutes political authority to regulate heresy. Luther answers definitively: "Heresy can never be restrained by force. . . . Heresy is a spiritual matter which you cannot hack to pieces with iron, consume with fire, or drown with water. God's word alone avails here."[8]

By 1530 Luther had changed his mind on this very important point and it had especially atrocious consequences in 1543. Because the Jews in Germany had publicly rejected Jesus' divinity and thus violated the Second Commandment against blasphemy, he recommended to the princes that they use their office and the sword by burning the Jews' synagogues and schools, destroying their houses, confiscating their books, forbidding their rabbis to teach, abolishing all rights of safe conduct, prohibiting their banking businesses, forcing them to do manual labor, and doing anything else necessary, short of killing, to "rid" Germany of Jews.[9] The error and evil of

Luther's violation of his 1523 theological political ethics remain beyond dispute! Four hundred years later Hitler used Luther's violation to recruit Lutherans for his murderous "final solution," even though Luther's argument against theocracy could have given Lutherans ample reason to resist Hitler.

At other times Luther upheld his rejection of theocracy even in the face of the emperor and the pope. One poignant case was the question whether the emperor should go to "war against the Turk." In *On War against the Turk* (1529) Luther vehemently resisted any holy war against the Muslim Ottoman Empire "as though our people were an army of Christians against the Turks, who were enemies of Christ. This is absolutely contrary to Christ's doctrine and name." It would be "idolatry and blasphemy. . . . Think of all the heartbreak and misery that have been caused by the *cruciata* [the Crusades], by the indulgences [that Pope Urban II granted to crusaders], and by crusade taxes."[10]

Luther could support a war against the Ottomans only if it were waged according to just-war criteria. Therefore, it would have to be waged under the legitimate authority of the emperor and princes and not under the auspices of, or as a cover for, the pope, the bishops, and the church. Moreover, it would have to be waged in order to protect the Empire from an expansionist war started by the Ottomans. Luther did not doubt that the Ottomans wanted to wage such a war, but he also had no doubt that past Holy Roman emperors and princes desired "to go to war for [reasons] such as the winning of great honor, glory, and wealth, the extension of territory, or wrath and revenge and other such reasons." Finally, Luther argued that any just war waged with the Ottomans would have to begin "with repentance" because of the crusades and the general history of waging "war-realism" wars. Luther urged Christians to lead the empire in repentance.[11]

Luther's rejection of holy war/crusade is an unmistakable contribution to JWT. John Calvin, however, the first theologian of the Reformed Protestant traditions, reintroduced Augustine's more theocratic holy-war rationale. This would plague Protestant thinking on war for centuries. Indeed, Calvin's influence still shapes the theocratic holy-war inclinations of certain right-wing Protestant movements in the twentieth and twenty-first centuries.

Fourth, Luther introduced what today we call selective conscientious objection, that is, to object to a particular war because of conscience. In 1520 he combined the Fifth Commandment's "Thou shalt not kill" with Peter's clause, "We must obey God rather than human authority" (Acts 5:29).

> But if, as often happens, the temporal power and authorities, or whatever they call themselves, would compel a subject to do something contrary to the command of God, or hinder him from doing what God commands, obedience ends and the obligation ceases. . . . [It is] as if a prince desired to go to war, and his cause was clearly unrighteous; we should neither follow nor help such a prince, because God had commanded us not to kill our neighbor or do him a wrong. . . . In such cases we should indeed give up our property and honor, our life and limb, so that God's commandments remain.[12]

These are the beginnings of what is often called Lutheran resistance theory, which has become even more important in our own more democratic times. We will take up Luther's fifth and sixth contributions to the tradition—a strong affirmation of social justice and the notion of public accountability—in chapter 6.

Vitoria

Francisco de Vitoria was a Spanish Roman Catholic contemporary of Luther. In addition to the Ottoman Empire, the other big international concern of medieval Christianity was the 1492 "discovery" of the New World. New questions about war and imperial expansion arose. In this context Vitoria made four contributions to JWT. He examined in detail the criterion of just cause and judged, first, that imperial expansion violated just cause, and second, that holy war/crusade likewise violated just cause. Third, he introduced a new element into the criteria of legitimate authority. Finally, he undertook the first ordered and extensive investigation of *in bello* criteria, which had only been randomly addressed previously.

Between 1539 and 1541 Emperor Charles V sought Vitoria's opinion on three questions. First, what property rights do the Indians in the New World have relative to the Spanish conquistadors? Second, what rights do Spanish rulers have over the Indians regarding civil law? And third, what rights do Spanish rulers and the Church have relative to the Indians' spiritual and religious life? Vitoria responded in two books, *On the Indians* and *On the Law of War*.

Vitoria noted that while the common law of nations recognizes that land that has no owner belongs to the one who discovers it, the "new world" lands claimed by Spain going all the way back to King Ferdinand and Queen Isabella were already "under a master [the Indians], and therefore do not come under the head of discovery." He rejected arguments that the Indians were either slaves or heretics or lacked a rational nature and were thereby unable to own land. He also rejected the notion that the emperor was the lord of the whole world and thus its owner. He thereby reasserted and clarified what Cicero had argued, that imperial expansion was not a just cause for waging war. "There is a single and only just cause for commencing a war, namely, a wrong received."[13] And this wrong must be based on natural law, like that embodied either in the second table of the Ten Commandments or in *jus gentium*—the law of nations. In this way Vitoria bravely and prophetically criticized Spanish imperial-war realism. He even convinced Emperor Charles V not to engage in holy war against the "new world" Indians.

Vitoria also rejected the proposition that the pope has temporal political authority and thus could use the sword to convert Indians.

He emphatically rejected waging war as punishment for either unbelief or blasphemy. "And it receives manifest confirmation from the fact . . . that, even if the barbarians refuse to accept Christ as their lord, this does not justify making war on them or doing them any hurt." And again, "Further, war is no argument for the truth of the Christian faith. Therefore the Indians cannot be induced by war to believe, but rather to feign belief and reception of the Christian faith, which is monstrous and a sacrilege." Emphatically he said, "Difference of religion is not a cause of just war."[14]

Vitoria noted that a legitimate political authority could wage a just war if it were absolutely necessary. Necessity might include the need to protect the natural right of Indians who had come to the faith if their right to do so were being denied by other Indians or Indian sovereigns. Necessity also might include the need to secure the natural right of Indians to hear the gospel voluntarily. A just war to protect the natural right of religious freedom cannot be waged, however, as a cover for a holy war/crusade to extend the Christian faith.[15]

Vitoria's third contribution to JWT was an important new insight regarding legitimate authority. While he recognized that a legitimate sovereign was the only one with the *right to declare* a justifiable war as the tradition had always held, he also argued that others had a *right to discern* whether the sovereign *ought* to declare war.

There is a doubtful point in connection with the justice of a war, whether it be enough for a just war that the prince believes himself to have a just cause. On this point let my first proposition be: This belief is not always enough. And for proof I rely, first, on the fact that in some matters of less moment it is not enough either for a prince or for private persons to believe that they are acting justly. This is notorious, for their error may be vincible and deliberate, and the opinion of the individual is not enough to render an act good, but it must come up to the standard of a wise man's judgment, as appears from [Aristotle's] *Ethics*, book 2. Also the result would otherwise be that very many wars would be just on both sides, for although it is not a common occurrence for princes to wage war in bad faith, they nearly always think theirs is a just cause.[16]

In this way Vitoria introduced a protocol for a system of checks and balances. Over the centuries this protocol eventually led to more constitutional and even democratic forms of legitimate authority, and ultimately to a system of international law. He also raised the issue of the possibility of selective conscientious objection against serving in a particular war that is manifestly unjust, though he did not forthrightly resolve the question.

Fourth, Vitoria examined in detail the situation of noncombatants and the treatment of prisoners of war. In this way he paved the way for the *jus in bello* criteria of noncombatant discrimination and proportionality of means, even though today we would not agree with him on each of his judgments on these matters.[17] By considering JWT in light of the European discovery of new-world nations, Vitoria prepared the ground for our last two transforming footprints.

Grotius

Hugo Grotius not only read Vitoria's work on just war in light of the newly discovered Indian nations, but he also anticipated the coming new era of intensified international relations. Without distaining earlier JWT, he desired above all to prepare it for future challenges. This was his first of six contributions to modernize the tradition.

Much of Europe was in the midst of the exceedingly bloody religious war, the Thirty Years' War (1618–1648), which killed over half the population in some countries. European Christendom was intensely politically fragmented along Catholic, Lutheran, and Calvinist confessional lines. Grotius was disgusted. "Throughout the Christian world I observed a lack of restraint in relation to war, such as even barbarous races should be ashamed of . . ."[18] In 1625, Grotius wrote *On the Law of War and Peace*, introducing an understanding of international law that would prevail from the 1648 Treaty of Westphalia, which ended the religious wars, until the present. This is the "Westphalian era" and its three international principles still prevail: sovereign nation-states have the right of political self-determination; all states have equal legal standing regarding self-determination; and ordinarily no state may intervene in the internal affairs of another state.[19]

Second, Grotius set just-war reasoning firmly, and for all practical purposes exclusively, upon a natural-law basis. He therefore softened JWT's reliance upon Scripture, Christian faith, and the church fathers, even though he himself thoroughly knew these authorities. He signaled his natural-law approach by citing Cicero in the second paragraph of his introduction—the "Prolegomena"—to his book. When the ancient Romans appealed to natural law in the context of international relations, they called it *jus gentium*, "law of the nations," a kind of agreement among many or all nations about some fundamental moral insight. Such broadly based agreements signaled, but did not guarantee, that the agreed-upon moral insight was rooted in the moral natural law, established either by Nature or Nature's God, as they liked to put it. All moral law is rooted in justice that itself serves the natural human desire to live a richer, more peaceable social life than any of the animals can have. This is true on the level of relations between states as well, for a "state is a complete association of free men, joined together for the enjoyment of rights and for their common interest."[20]

By establishing JWT on the basis of the law of nations, Grotius opposed the war-realist reasons for waging war—like gaining advantage, honor, glory, or a meaningful life —whether God existed or not. With this modern secularized (that is, nontheological) approach he also sought to counter the desire to wage the kind of interconfessional holy war that raged not only in his time but also periodically over the next 150 years: "What we have been saying would have a degree of validity even if we should concede that which cannot be conceded without the utmost wickedness, that there is no God, or that the affairs of men are of no concern to Him. . . . Thus God Himself suffers Himself to be judged according to this [natural law] standard, as may be seen by referring to Genesis 18:25; Isaiah 5:3; Ezekiel 18:25; Jeremiah 2:9; Micah 6:2; Romans 2:6 and 3:6."[21]

Third, Grotius focused intently on just cause according to natural law. In this way, too, he disputed the justifiability of the religious wars of his time. Only self-defense is a truly justifiable cause for waging war. This is true even though, along with self-defense, he included the two other traditional justifiable causes, that is, recovery of property or debt and punishment for a committed offense. But he included these latter traditional reasons as virtual subcategories of self-defense. This minimized their independent status as justifiable reasons for going to war. Later generations would confirm his point by eliminating recovery and punishment altogether.[22]

By turning to the law of nations in the light of the new modern international situation, in his fourth contribution Grotius promoted legitimate authority on the basis of a modern concept of sovereignty. In medieval JWT, up through Luther and Vitoria, the prince received his legitimate authority from above, so to speak, that is, as God's minister. The prince's authority manifested itself in the prince's personal moral character under God. A prince was the head of the body, disciplining and directing it from above for its own good. In Grotius's secularized law-of-nations approach, rulers receive their legitimate authority from below, from the state composed of associated free persons. As also sovereign authority belongs to the whole body politic with the government as the body's particular organ for legitimate power. He used this analogy in order to provide a basis for legitimate authority as if God did not exist![23]

With this modern concept of sovereignty, Grotius made a fifth contribution to modern JWT. Public procedures hold the government (the eye) accountable to the wider state (the body politic). These public procedures therefore take the place traditionally occupied by the prince's personal moral character under God. A ruler's own subjective right intention plays a lesser role in favor of international public accountability, what is called "publicity."

On this basis Grotius made a public declaration of war an important ingredient for waging a just war. The purpose is not so much to warn the enemy, as had been the case in ancient and medieval times. Rather, the public declaration keeps the state who wages war accountable to third-party nations under the law of nations:

> Declarations of war in fact . . . were wont to be made publicly, with a statement of the cause, in order that the whole human race as it were might judge of the justness of it. Of a truth wisdom is the virtue characteristic of the ruler, as it seemed to Aristotle also, but justice is the virtue characteristic of a [that is, every] man, in so far as he is a man.

In this way Grotius intensified Vitoria's point about the distinction between the right to declare and the right to discern a justifiable war, and expanded it to include the international community of nation-states.[24]

Grotius's turn toward international publicity provided five needed safeguards. (1) It ensures that justice is the real basis for waging war as punishment. "Finally . . . we must add this word of warning, that wars which are undertaken to inflict punishment are under suspicion of being unjust, unless crimes are very atrocious and very evident . . ." Passing the international publicity test for "very atrocious and very evident" crimes strictly limits a powerful nation's temptation to be the sole avenger of wrong. (2) International publicity pertains to a potential preemptive war against a threatening enemy. Preemptive war "is permissible only when the danger is immediate and certain, not when it is merely assumed." Third parties will sniff out the inordinate fear one state might have about the assumed wicked intentions and capabilities of another nation. Inordinate fear, noted Grotius, often leads to unjust wars purported to be preemptive. (3) International publicity exposes the injustice of a so-called "preventive war," which seeks to prevent another state from someday possibly becoming an armed aggressor. "But that the possibility of being attacked confers the right to attack is abhorrent to every principle of equity," argued Grotius. As a category "preventive war" exhibits a permissive moral laxity from the perspective of JWT. Preventive wars are indistinguishable from war realism. Here is a prime example of alien expectations that are subtly and inexcusably transferred into JWT. (4) International publicity exposes the unjust pretentiousness of self-styled civilized and benevolent nations who desire to civilize others through either threatening or waging war. Approvingly, Grotius quoted the ancient natural law philosopher Plutarch: "To wish to impose civilization upon uncivilized peoples is a pretext which may serve to conceal greed for what is another's." Such "civilizing wars" are another form of war realism, are a kind of secularized holy war/crusade, and are the backbone of self-styled benevolent empires. Again, they exemplify alien expectations that are subtly and inexcusably transferred into JWT. (5) International publicity lends perspective for weighing the proportionality of ends.[25]

Grotius's principle of publicity led him to introduce into modern JWT the notion of conscientious objection to participating in an unjust war. While Luther and Vitoria had the makings of conscientious objection, Grotius made it a feature of JWT. Vitoria, for instance, did not morally oblige a common citizen to judge the justifiability of a particular war. Common people were simply to trust their ruler's competence to declare war and to obey their ruler's declaration. By doing so, common people themselves were not culpable if the war were not justifiably waged. The ruler is culpable for waging an unjust war but a foot soldier is not. The general population, therefore, can support troops without supporting the unjust war itself or the ruler who declared it.

Grotius was more proactive about conscientious objection. "If those under the rule of another are ordered to take the field, as often occurs, they should altogether refrain from so doing; if it is clear to them that the cause of the war is unjust." He then quoted Peter's clause in Acts 5:29 ("We must obey God rather than human authority"), followed by a host of authorities—other Scriptures, Christian and Jewish theologians, and Greco-Roman philosophers.[26]

Grotius's principle of publicity has not gone unnoticed. The founders of the United States, for instance, knew it well and took it to heart. Thomas Jefferson inscribed international publicity into the opening paragraph of the *Declaration of Independence*: ". . . a decent respect to the opinions of mankind requires that they should declare the causes which impel them to the separation."

Sixth, Grotius united in a single work the two parts of JWT, *jus ad bellum* and *jus in bello*. After Grotius, war is *always judged twice*. He dedicated an entire volume of his three-volume work to the conduct of war in a justifiable manner. He thereby responded to the new, more destructive and totalistic systems of weaponry available in his time. He therefore began his *in bello* treatment with proportionality of means.

Grotius rehearsed countless cases throughout the law of nations where the right to kill, pillage, and destroy is unrestrained. Ingeniously, he then presented an extensive counterargument based upon the moral natural law of moderation and proportionality: "An enemy therefore who wishes to observe, not what the laws of men permit, but what his duty requires, what is right from the point of view of religion and morals, will spare the blood of his foes; and will condemn no one to death, unless to save himself from death or some like evil . . ." Even in the case of an enemy "love for our neighbor prevents us from pressing our right to the utmost limit." Prisoners of war should be spared as well as those who surrender. Along the way he considered the complicated cases of deception and concluded that deception is generally justifiable except when making promises, accepting conditions of surrender, signing treaties, taking oaths to assure the safety of hostages or enemy soldiers, or the like.[27]

After dealing with proportionality Grotius considered the general noncombatant immunity of civilians.

> Again, with regard to the destruction of those who are killed by accident and without intent, we must hold fast to the principle which we mentioned above. It is the bidding of mercy, if not of justice, that, except for reasons that are weighty and will affect the safety of many, no action should be attempted whereby innocent persons may be threatened with destruction.[28]

Grotius concluded his thinking about *jus in bello* with an extensive treatment of the natural law of good faith between enemies in order to bring about a lasting peace. A state must maintain good faith even if the other party is faithless.

> And good faith should be preserved, not only for other reasons but also in order that the hope of peace may not be done away with. For not only is every state sustained by good faith, as Cicero declares, but also that greater society of states. Aristotle truly says that, if good faith has been taken away, 'all intercourse among men ceases to exist.'[29]

Grotius's contributions to JWT caught the attention of the warring nations already by the early 1630s. King Gustavus Adolphus of Sweden carried Grotius's writings in his saddlebags as he led his Lutheran troops into battle. Grotius's influence grew continuously over the next three centuries. The Napoleonic wars (1805–1815) severely strained the Westphalian era of international law among sovereign nations. Napoleon Bonaparte thought that the French ideals of liberty, equality, and fraternity were universal values and that he had the calling to spread these ideals across Europe at gunpoint. But the Congress of Vienna (1815) and the Treaty of Paris (1815) put the Westphalian era and its law-of-nations approach to war and peace back on course. This was a clear rejection of war in the service of an empire even when the ideals appear noble.

International Humanitarian Law and the United Nations

The middle of the nineteenth century gave rise to increasing interest in the international law of war, eventually to be called "International Humanitarian Law" (hereafter IHL). In 1859, Jean-Henri Dunant (1828–1910), a Swiss businessman and social activist, witnessed the Battle of Solferino, where within ten hours 5,500 soldiers were killed and over 23,000 were wounded. He saw many wounded and incapacitated soldiers merely bayoneted by the opposing army, and he himself took care of hundreds of wounded survivors. In 1863 he organized "The Committee of Five," which included himself and the representatives of four other leading families of Geneva, Switzerland. In 1901 the first Nobel Peace Prize was awarded to Dunant.

"The Committee of Five" organized an international conference in October 1863 attended by thirty-six representatives, including official representatives of eighteen European countries. This was the founding of the International Committee of the Red Cross (ICRC), as it has been known since 1876. The ICRC now includes the Red Crescent, the Red Lion and Sun, and the Red Crystal emblems in order to institutionalize its nondiscriminatory character. The ICRC movement began by focusing on the right of all soldiers to medical attention and the right of medical and relief personnel to noncombatant immunity. In 1864 the Swiss government invited all the

European states as well as the United States, Brazil, and Mexico to attend a convention in Geneva where twelve states and kingdoms—not the United States—adopted the first Geneva Convention "for the Amelioration of the Condition of the Wounded in Armies in the Field." Here for the first time modern nation-states ratified a written law of war. In April 1863 the United States instituted *General Orders No. 100*, usually called the Lieber Code. The Lieber Code was the first codification of *jus in bello* principles. While it was only internal to the United States, it helped to inspire an international movement to convene the Hague Conventions of 1899 and 1907.[30]

The Hague Conventions adopted the 1864 Geneva Convention and its tradition of *jus in bello* law, and the United States and many other nations ratified them. They established IHL for maritime and aerial warfare; recognized the basic human dignity and civil rights of prisoners of war; prohibited the use of certain gruesome weapons technology including chemical weapons of mass destruction; ratified the *jus ad bellum* criterion of public declaration of war thus promoting the principle of publicity; and established the Permanent Court of Arbitration, housed in the Peace Palace in The Hague, Netherlands. The Permanent Court of Arbitration is one way to institutionalize the principle of publicity and the *jus ad bellum* criterion of last resort.[31]

On July 26, 1945, in San Francisco, California, fifty nation-states signed the United Nations Charter. The Charter's Preamble reads:

We the peoples of the United Nations determined

to save succeeding generations from the scourge of war, which in our lifetime has brought untold sorrow to mankind, and

to reaffirm faith in fundamental human rights, in the dignity and worth of the human person, in the equal rights of men and women and of nations large and small, and to establish conditions under which justice and respect for the obligations arising from treaties and other sources of international law can be maintained, and

to promote social progress and better standards of life in larger freedom . . .

have resolved to combine our efforts to accomplish these aims.[32]

Article 2 of the UN Charter confirms the Westphalian principle of sovereign, equal, and inviolable nation-states: "The Organization is based on the principle of the sovereign equality of all its Members." Articles 24 and 39–40 establish the Security Council as the key but not sole agent of publicity in reference to public declaration. Article 41 recognizes last resort and Article 42 authorizes the Security Council to initiate necessary collective armed action against an aggressor nation-state. Articles 43–50 implement the armed actions.

Finally, Article 51 recognizes the right of self-defense and, indeed, consciously and stringently restricts just cause to self-defense alone.

Nothing in the present Charter shall impair the inherent right of individual or collective self-defense if an armed attack occurs against a Member of the United Nations, until the Security Council has taken measures necessary to maintain international peace and security. Measures taken by Members in the exercise of this right of self-defense shall be immediately reported to the Security Council and shall not in any way affect the authority and responsibility of the Security Council under the present Charter to take at any time such action as it deems necessary in order to maintain or restore international peace and security.

Planning, preparing, initiating, or waging a war of aggression are all "crimes against peace." Restricting just cause to defense is the major contribution to *jus ad bellum* provided by the United Nations and IHL.[33]

In 1949 the United Nations convened four Geneva Conventions. One hundred ninety-four nation-states have now ratified the Geneva Conventions along with their three Additional Protocols. Together these form the core of IHL and *jus in bello*. Five key features make up the Geneva Conventions and the Additional Protocols: the principle of noncombatant immunity; the use of proportional means that minimize the unnecessary loss of life or excessive suffering of soldiers; the recognition of the basic human dignity and legal rights of prisoners of war; the recognition of the basic human dignity and civil rights of civilians within occupied territories; and the fiduciary and protective role of the ICRC.[34]

IHL sustains the moral worth of all parties to a conflict and strengthens the good faith needed in order to reach a measure of justice and a sustainable "end of peace," as Grotius knew so well. IHL's focus on proportionality of means therefore bars the taking of hostages and scorched-earth tactics with respect to an enemy's physical or cultural property; prohibits at any time and place all affronts to the human dignity of a prisoner of war, like humiliating or degrading treatment or pubic curiosity of an enemy's body or character, slander of an enemy's family or nation, and blasphemy of an enemy's religion; and outlaws unnatural cruelty, rape, disfiguration, mutilation, torture, ethnic cleansing, and genocide. These various "war crimes" and "crimes against humanity" have now become the international benchmarks for conduct in war.

Our basic "footprints" end here. In part three we will explore several ongoing challenges of JWT from the perspective of the Christian faith and in light of the contemporary world situation of nations and empires. We will see how JWT within the rich arc of just peacemaking continues to develop IHL for the global common good.

Questions for reflection and discussion

1. In what ways do you and don't you see Luther's "two-kingdom" theology as a realistic perspective for Christians to take toward government today? How do you see this theology being supported or violated in contemporary affairs?

2. Luther said, "Heresy can never be restrained by force," yet he later violated this very point in calling for ridding Germany of Jews. Do you see any contemporary parallel dangers in, for instance, the involvement of the so-called religious right in political affairs?

3. Grotius moved away from the Western Christendom practice of explicitly naming the biblical God and citing the Holy Bible as explicit warrants for his natural law approach to the just-war tradition. What advantages or disadvantages do you see in this shift of perspective?

4. Over the course of the Iraq War, the reasons for going to battle have shifted. How do you think Grotius's principle of publicity might apply today to democratic citizenship and to the responsibilities of nation-states within the international community? How do you think Grotius's assertions of "conscientious objector" status might apply to soldiers who conclude that the war is unjust?

5. International Humanitarian Law and the Geneva Conventions strictly prohibit torture, yet the United States has challenged what constitutes torture. Do you think that the unpredictable and violent nature of terrorism changes how we should interpret those international standards?

Part Three

God's Preferential Future for Earthly Peace

5

Reconsidering Just-War Tradition and Pacifism

As we have already seen, JWT Christians respond to the pacifism question in a dynamic, twofold way. As a confessional church the Lutheran voice bases faith and life on God's two ways of ruling the world according to law and gospel. On the one hand, therefore, faith understands that Christian love renounces the authority of "the sword" and other forms of force and violence in matters of the gospel within churchly life and in matters where one's own faith and life are primarily at stake. On the other hand, faith understands that in Christian love we participate in political authority and its powers because God institutes and constrains them by moral law for the protection and peace of all creation.

Still, the horrendous violence of war over the last 150 years has led Christians again to confront the questions of violence and war in the light of God's preferential future for earthly peace. Two different trajectories have emerged. The pacifist trajectory renounces the violence of war. The International Humanitarian Law trajectory legally restricts and restrains war's violence according to broadly agreed-upon moral insights aimed at keeping, restoring, or establishing peace with justice.

But stating the matter in this way is shortsighted in two ways. First, pacifists not only *renounce* violence, but they also *announce* peace and practice just peacemaking. Second, people of the International Humanitarian Law trajectory not only restrict and restrain violence and war, but they too announce and practice just peacemaking as the preferred way of peacekeeping. In this chapter we will explore how Roman Catholics have reconsidered these matters.

The strong presumption against war

In 1983, the U.S. Conference of Catholic Bishops issued *The Challenge of Peace*, its influential pastoral letter on war and peace. The letter begins with the bishops agreeing with the Second Vatican Council (1962–1965), "The whole human race faces a moment of supreme crisis in its advance toward maturity. . . . Since the council, the dynamic of the nuclear arms race has intensified. Apprehension about nuclear war is almost tangible and visible today."[1]

The bishops start their "Summary" provocatively: "Catholic teaching begins in every case with a presumption against war and for the peaceful settlement of disputes."[2] They base this "presumption" on the natural-law principle to "do no harm." Later they note that the decision to go to war must meet rigorous conditions: "Such a decision, especially today, requires extraordinarily strong reasons for overriding the presumption *in favor of peace* and *against* war" (emphasis in the original).

In 1993, the bishops commemorated the tenth anniversary of *The Challenge of Peace* by publishing *The Harvest of Justice Is Sown in Peace*. At least seven devastating regional armed conflicts had taken place in the ensuing decade. Here the bishops upped the ante by upholding the "strong presumption" against the use of force.[3]

Why this very muscular language of "strong presumption against war"? JWT had never before used such a potent phrase. At least four factors gave rise to it. First, there was the "almost tangible and visible apprehension" of a gathering danger of nuclear holocaust. A second, similar factor was the rapid development, proliferation, and even use of biological and chemical weapons of mass destruction, as well as of the new technologically sophisticated "conventional" weaponry. A third factor was the posture of many modern nation-states, especially the superpowers and aspiring superpowers, which aroused suspicions of their general arrogance, self-interestedness, hardness, and even maliciousness. Fourth, the first three factors led a swelling number of Catholics, both lay and religious, to join a century-long emerging movement of new pacifism.

This Catholic turn toward pacifism found nourishment in a century of papal statements going back to Pope Pius IX and the First Vatican Council in the 1870s. Then, in 1963, right in the midst of the Second Vatican Council, Pope John XXIII issued his encyclical *Pacem in Terris—Peace on Earth*. It was a blockbuster in the eyes of the Catholic pacifist movement.

Pacem in Terris condemns the Cold War arms race. The arms race leads nations to outspend one another constantly based on "a common belief that under modern conditions peace cannot be assured except on the basis of an equal balance of armaments." *Pacem in Terris* admits that the arms race "does indeed act as a deterrent," but it is fear based and leads to the spiraling stockpile of nuclear and conventional armaments. The "vast outlay" of resources has "saddled [countries] with a great burden," which prevents them from improving the economic and social development of their own nation and of others. This military drain of resources is the very definition of militarism. The Second Vatican Council issued a similar condemnation: "The arms race is one of the greatest curses on the human race and the harm it inflicts upon the poor is more than can be endured."[4]

To "abolish" militarism, argued Pope John XXIII, "requires that the fundamental principles upon which peace is based in today's world be replaced by an altogether different one, namely, the realization that true and lasting peace among nations [can be based] . . . only in mutual trust." Then came the Pope's *coup de grâce* to JWT. "Thus, in this age which boasts of its atomic power, it no longer makes sense to maintain that war is a fit instrument with which to repair the violation of justice." The Second Vatican Council agreed, "All these factors force us to undertake a completely fresh reappraisal of war."[5]

There is a variety of pacifisms, and the Pope's kind—he never used the word—is a version of "pragmatic (or consequentialist) pacifism," which is distinct from "principled (or pure) pacifism." Principled pacifism opposes violence and war in principle, no matter what the situation is or the circumstances are. The principle itself comes from some ultimate authority. For Christian principled pacifists, like the Mennonites, Quakers, Brethren, and Amish, the authority is Jesus. Principled pacifism starts with a pure presumption against war. Modern pragmatic pacifism, on the other hand, weighs the general overall state of the world and the indiscriminant destructiveness of modern weaponry. So-called nuclear pacifism is a form of pragmatic pacifism. Pragmatic pacifists conclude on this basis that violence and war inevitably unleash way more evil than they produce good. Violence only breeds more violence, is a common assessment. Pragmatic pacifism holds an exceedingly strong presumption against war.

The Challenge of Peace sounds a lot like *Pacem in Terris*. In order to unite the "many voices . . . and multiple forms of religious witness" the bishops note "a common presumption against the use of force as a means of settling disputes." They also sense a "new moment." They strive to stimulate a fruitful conversation between JWT and pacifist traditions without papering over their differences. They invite all Catholics to develop a theology of peace that would ground just peacemaking. And again they cite the Second Vatican Council: "Peace is not merely the absence of war. . . . Instead, it is rightly and appropriately called "an enterprise of justice" (Isa. 32:17).[6]

The Harvest of Justice Is Sown in Peace expands Catholic just peacemaking. Here the bishops affirm the unity within diversity of JWT and pacifism by focusing on the vocation, virtues, vision, and agenda of just peacemaking.

Entering an era of new global interdependencies

In both pastoral letters the U.S. Cathoic bishops respond "to the duty of scrutinizing the signs of the times." They are mindful of a new era:

> Just as the nation-state was a step in the evolution of government at a time when expanding trade and new weapons technologies made the feudal system inadequate to manage the resulting conflicts and provide security, so we are now entering an era of new, global interdependencies requiring global systems of governance to manage the resulting conflicts and ensure our common security.[7]

The bishops look especially toward the UN as a sign of new possibilities in the world. They affirm Pope Paul VI's 1965 opinion about the UN: "The edifice which you have constructed must never fail; it must be perfected and made equal to the needs which world history will present. You mark a stage in the development of mankind for which retreat must never be admitted, but from which it is necessary that advance be made."[8] This puts the bishops within the trajectory of International Humanitarian Law, though with a strong presumption in favor of just peacemaking.

The bishops promote the UN without advocating one world government, without overlooking the UN's limitations and flaws, and without turning a blind eye to needed changes. They are not utopians but gradualist progressives in the spirit of Pope John XXIII:

> There are indeed some people who, in their generosity of spirit, burn with a desire to institute wholesale reforms whenever they come across situations which show scant regard for justice or are wholly out of keeping with its claims. They tackle the problem with such impetuosity that one would think they were embarking on some political revolution.
>
> We would remind such people that it is the law of nature that all things must be of gradual growth. If there is to be any improvement in human institutions, the work must be done slowly and deliberatively from within.[9]

In our next chapter we will explore Lutheran reasons for a unified theology of peace.

Questions for reflection and discussion

1. Do you relate more to the pacifist trajectory or the IHL trajectory? Why?
2. The Catholic Bishops' "strong presumption against war" cites four factors, including nuclear arms proliferation, as giving rise to this strong language. Do you think these same dangers continue today? Are there new dangers not cited here?
3. How do you think the UN can help promote just peacemaking? What are its limitations?

6

A Lutheran Unified Theology of Earthly Peace

A Lutheran unified theology of earthly peace confirms Lutheranism's confessional heritage about JWT but places it within a broader theology of earthly peace and a more encompassing practice of just peacemaking. A unified approach both prioritizes just peacemaking and decisively distinguishes JWT from war realism and holy war/crusade. Moreover, it affirms "the strong presumption against war" as it helps to overcome the popular confusion of war realism with JWT, especially in light of the United States' superpower status. As already noted, war-realism expectations are routinely transferred to JWT. "The strong presumption against war" minimizes this malignant transference, whether it is made intentionally or not.

We will travel five roads on our way to a Lutheran unified theology of peace. First, we will explore Luther's theological and ethical reflections on the office of the prince relative to justice and peacemaking. Second, we will explore his reflections on the office of the prince and the principle of publicity. Third, we will look at a contemporary ecumenical approach to just peacemaking. Fourth, we will look briefly at tried and true Lutheran just peacemaking and identify a Lutheran "pacific turn" as we meet new challenges. Finally, we will conclude with a brief meditation on the notion of "every church a peace church."

Luther on just peacemaking

For Luther a necessary justifiable war fulfills the duty to protect. He does not, however, stop there! Rather, he expands the duties of the office of the prince to include what today we call just peacemaking. In his catechisms he includes both duties within the Fifth Commandment's "Thou shalt not kill."

> This commandment is violated not only when we do evil, but also when we have the opportunity to do good to our neighbors and to prevent, protect, and save them from suffering bodily harm or injury, but fail to do so. If you send a naked person away when you could clothe him, you have let him freeze to death. If you see anyone who is suffering from hunger and do not feed her, you have let her starve. Likewise, if you see anyone who is condemned to death or in similar peril and do not save him although you have means and ways to do so, you have killed him. It will be of no help for you to use the excuse that you did not assist their deaths by word or deed, for you have withheld your love from them and robbed them of the kindness by means of which their lives might have been saved.
>
> Therefore God rightly calls all persons murderers who do not offer counsel or assistance to those in need and peril of body and life.[1]

Ambrose's maxim lives in Luther. The negative "thou shalt not" acts as a protective boundary while the implied positive "thou shalt" acts as a life-generating bridge. Building boundaries and bridges both belong to the prince's office. In this way Luther departs significantly from Augustine's heritage of reducing earthly peace to the mere "solace of our misery." Indeed, Luther confesses that God as creator continually desires a goodly measure of positive enjoyment of earthly felicity even in the face of sin and evil.

On several occasions Luther composed a "mirror of the prince," a common form of literature that a respected person of moral wisdom, like a theologian, would write as instruction for a prince or another kind of political official. The prince was to look into this mirror upon rising each morning, see what a righteous prince was to look like, and then go and do likewise.

Luther composed his most famous "mirror" based upon Psalm 82. Here he combines this psalm with the standard JWT text (Rom. 13:1-4) for legitimate authority. He also connects his mirror with Jehoshaphat's teaching to rulers in 2 Chronicles 19:6: "Consider what you are doing, for you judge not on behalf of human beings but on the Lord's behalf." Psalm 82 begins, "God stands in the congregation of God/and is Judge among the gods" (v. 1, translation from Luther's Works: American Edition).

The "gods" are God's earthly representatives deputized by God for political rule and the "congregation" is any earthly city. While Luther also includes a mirror for those who are ruled, he focuses here on the prince's mirror. He turns again to Jehoshaphat who instructs the "gods" in "the fear of the LORD": "Now, let the fear of the LORD be upon you; take care what you do, for there is no perversion of justice with the Lord our God, or partiality, or taking of bribes" (2 Chron. 19:7). "The fear of the LORD" is the biblical language for accountability to God.

Luther continues:

> But neither are the gods to be proud and self-willed. For they are not gods among the people and overlords of the congregation in such a way that they have this position all to themselves and can do as they like. Not so! God Himself is there also. He will judge, punish, and correct them; and if they do not obey, they will not escape. . . . He keeps down the rulers, so that they do not abuse His majesty and power according to their own

self-will but use them for that peace for which He has appointed and preserves them.[2]

Luther eloquently extols God's care for earthly cities:

Observe that he [Moses] calls all communities or organized assemblies "the congregation of God," because they are God's own, and He accepts them as His own work, just as (Jonah 3:3) He calls Nineveh "a city of God." For He has made, and makes, all communities. He still brings them together, feeds them, lets them grow, blesses and preserves them, gives them fields and meadows, cattle, water, air, sun and moon, and everything they have, even body and life, as it is written (Gen. 1:29). . . .

Such communities are God's work, which He daily creates, supports, and increases, so that they can sit at home and beget children and educate them. Therefore this word is, in the first place, a great and pleasant comfort to all those who find themselves situated in such a community. It assures them that God accepts them as His work and His creation, cares for them and protects and supports them, as we can, in fact, see with our own eyes. . . . For this word "congregation of God" is a precious word.[3]

Political authority rules in God's stead for the sake of the city. They are, therefore, accountable to God, and justice and peacemaking are the standards. Consider the next three verses of Psalm 82:

How long will you judge unjustly
>And prefer the persons of the godless?
Judge the poor and the orphan
>And help the wretched and needy to justice.
Rescue the small and poor man,
>Deliver him out of the hand of the godless. (Ps. 82:2-4, translation from Luther's Works: American Edition)

Justice means, in Luther's words, "to help the poor, the orphans, and the widows to justice, and to further their cause. But, again, who can tell all the virtues that follow from this one? For this virtue includes all the works of righteousness."[4]

Luther uses the image of a "heavenly and divine hospital" to talk about the prince as just peacemaker. As such, the prince provides palliative care for the very poor by seeing that their needs are met. And he provides preventive care for rich and poor alike by preserving "living and goods" so that they need not fall into poverty. "For so to help a man that he does not need to become a beggar is just as much of a good work and a virtue and an alms as to give to a man and to help a man who has already become a beggar."[5]

Luther extols the prince as just peacemaker:

> In a word, after the Gospel or the ministry, there is on earth no better jewel, no greater treasure, nor richer alms, no fairer endowment, no finer possession than a ruler who makes and preserves just laws. Such men are rightly called gods. These are the virtues, the profit, the fruits, and the good works that God has appointed to this rank in life. It is not for nothing that He has called them gods; and it is not His will that it shall be a lazy, empty, idle estate, in which men seek honor, power, luxury, selfish profit, and self-will. He would have them full of great, innumerable, unspeakable good works, so that they may be partakers of His divine majesty and help Him to do divine and superhuman works.

In Western medieval civilization "the sword" is the symbol of defense and punishment, that is, retributive justice. "The scepter" is the symbol of the full range of justice and just peacemaking authoritatively encoded as law. Luther recognizes that the sword must be based in the scepter: "For this reason they [various rulers] are depicted on their seals with a book in one hand and a sword in the other, as a sign that they administer law and peace. Law is wisdom and should be the first of the two; for government by force without wisdom does not last." Luther concludes: "It is indeed a splendid and needful thing to build strong cities and castles against one's enemy; but that is nothing when compared with the work of a prince who builds a stronghold of peace."[6]

Luther on publicity

Luther was a forerunner of Grotius's principle of publicity. The mirror of a prince tradition was already a rudimentary form of publicity. Luther took this a step further when he stressed a prince's accountable to God. In the biblical imagination God ordinarily uses this-worldly means to do God's work, including God's work of holding political authorities accountable.

So, commenting on Psalm 82:1, Luther asks, "Where, then, is God?" Who is God's earthly agent for holding a prince accountable? For Luther it is priests and preachers, "to whom [God] has committed the duty of teaching, exhorting, rebuking, comforting, in a word, of preaching the Word of God."[7] God holds a prince accountable by making public admonition an aspect of the preaching office: because of the admonitory duty preachers are to stand in the city as God stands. "Observe, however, that a preacher by whom God rebukes the gods is to 'stand in the congregation.' He is to 'stand': that is, he is to be firm and confident and deal uprightly and honestly with it; and 'in the congregation,' that is, openly and boldly before God and men." Luther stresses the full publicity of such admonition:

> By this two sins are prevented. The first is unfaithfulness. There are many bishops and preachers in the ministry, but they do not "stand" and serve God faithfully. On the contrary, they lie down or otherwise play with their office. These are lazy and worthless preachers who do not tell the princes and lords their sins. In some cases they do not notice the sins. They lie down and snore in their

office and do nothing that pertains to it except that, like swine, they take up the room where good preachers should stand. These form the great majority. Others, however, play the hypocrite and flatter the wicked gods and strengthen them in their self-will. . . . Still others fear for their skins and are afraid that they must lose life and goods. All these do not "stand" and are not faithful to Christ.

The other sin is called backbiting. The whole world is full in every corner of preachers and laymen who bandy evil words about their gods, i.e., princes and lords, curse them, and call them names, though not boldly in the open, but in corners and in their own sects. But nothing is accomplished except to make the evil worse. It serves only to set a secret fire by which people are moved to disobedience, rebellion, breach of the peace, and contempt for their rulers. If you are in the ministry and are not willing to rebuke your gods openly and publicly, as your office demands, at least leave off your private backbiting, calling of names, criticizing, and complaining, or go hang! . . .

So, then, this first verse teaches that to rebuke rulers is not seditious, provided it is done in the way here described. . . . It would be far more seditious if a preacher did not rebuke the sins of the rulers; for then he makes people angry and sullen, strengthens the wickedness of the tyrants, becomes a partaker in it, and bears responsibility for it.[8]

Again, Luther draws from Ambrose's biblical maxim that sins of omission are the moral equivalent of sins of commission.

In 1534 Luther wrote a mirror of the prince for his own prince John Frederick, in which he identifies a second earthly agent of God's publicity, which he calls "extraordinary leaders." Sometimes these extraordinary leaders are themselves political rulers; most often they are not. They have "a special star before God" and are not so much trained or made as created and taught directly by God.

They possess a special measure of "natural law and natural reason." God raises up "such jewels, when, where, and to whom He pleases," "not only among His chosen people but also among the godless and the heathen; and not only in the ranks of the nobility but also among the middle classes, farmers, and laborers."[9]

Luther imagines these extraordinary leaders to be like random acts of God's publicity. God can even use one's enemies, whether or not they act justifiably, as agents of divine publicity. Indeed, God often uses one scoundrel to punish another, as Luther often quips. What Luther could not yet imagine was that God could raise up an entire new way of ruling that itself would provide the earthly means of God's publicity. Providing publicity is a key feature of more democratic ways of rule. The best democracies are deliberative ones, they are shot through with publicity.

Contemporary Christian just peacemaking

In 1992 a group of twenty-three Christian scholars and activists began meeting to think through the strengths, weakness, opportunities, threats, and challenges of just peacemaking. They came from both historic peace churches and historic just-war churches, from Roman Catholic traditions and from various Protestant traditions. Since that time countless others have joined this movement. They have come from congregations as well as synodical and denominational headquarters, from social-ministry and other civil-society organizations, from colleges and seminaries, and from countless other places of responsibility. Christians in this movement thoroughly acknowledge their many differences, including whether they have a pure presumption against war and are thus pacifist or whether they have a strong presumption against war and are thus JWT folks. Still, they have come to focus upon peace and to ponder and act upon the theology, theory, and practices of just peacemaking.

The original group proposed ten practices of this new ethic of just peacemaking,[10] which they then grouped around three biblical convictions about discipleship: (1) taking peacemaking initiatives, (2) advancing justice for all, and (3) strengthening the cooperative forces of love and community:

- Taking peacemaking initiatives:
    1. support nonviolent direction action;
    2. take independent initiatives to reduce threat;
    3. use cooperative conflict resolution; and
    4. acknowledge responsibility for conflict and injustice and seek repentance and forgiveness.

- Advancing justice for all:
    5. advance democracy, human rights, and religious liberty; and
    6. foster just and sustainable economic development.

- Strengthening the cooperative forces of love and community:
    7. work with emerging cooperative forces in the international system;
    8. strengthen the United Nations and international efforts for cooperation and human rights;
    9. reduce offensive weapons and weapons trade; and
    10. encourage grassroots peacemaking groups and voluntary associations.

Some people or congregations or groups of congregations concentrate entirely on one or two of these endeavors. Others may at various times, places, and circumstances engage in numerous practices. This list is not exhaustive and surely one practice in no way excludes engaging a different one. Furthermore, it is noteworthy that people, communities, and organizations that are not Christian engage in these practices!

A Lutheran "pacific turn"

Historically Lutherans have not used the term *just peacemaking* to describe what they do. But, we have in fact been engaging these practices since the time of Luther. The umbrella term *just peacemaking* can help us appreciate and retrieve a legacy that we have often let slip away. This legacy, like a mind, is a terrible thing to waste. Reclaiming this legacy will help make a "pacific turn," as tried and true Lutheran practices meet new challenges.[11]

For well over a century Lutherans and their congregations around the country have created institutions of many sizes and shapes for the protection and promotion of this, that, and the other thing related to the peace, justice, and wellness of communities, families, and persons. Most of these institutions have sprouted from the grassroots as Lutherans met the pressing needs of their communities, remembering that Christians live out their various vocations through institutions of one sort or another. Today many of these institutions are gathered under the umbrella of the alliance known as Lutheran Services in America (LSA).[12] According to LSA's mission statement, its member organizations "have an effective voice for service and justice to church, to government and to society." Effective voices for justice will always be deeply rooted in thick works of mercy and service. When mercy and justice kiss, just peacemaking thrives. Moreover, with the deep roots of LSA organizations in congregational life, the pacific turn toward Lutheran just peacemaking will increase with this mutual enrichment and collaborative companionship. Can we imagine and anticipate the time when collaborative companionship in just peacemaking becomes a prominent characteristic of Lutheran vocation? How can we extend this collaborative companionship to "civil society" as well?

In a deliberative democracy like ours the arena for just peacemaking is called "civil society." Civil society overlaps with other mega-arenas like politics, the economy, and family and friendships. Civil society is a vast and complex phenomenon and just peacemaking is one of its chief callings. When just peacemaking is in play, civil society becomes a sounding board and warning system for problems of justice, civil and human rights, freedom, and well-being. It defines the moral meaning of issues and frequently offers possible responses and solutions. It dramatizes predicaments and energizes possible responses for the broad citizenship as well as for government and the economy. It is the place for action that addresses injustice, oppression, and diminished well-being.

Just-peacemaking practices, institutions, and systems are the coin of the realm of civil society and make it indispensable for a thriving democratic culture. Just peacemaking makes civil society God's preferential arena for moral wisdom. It also makes civil society one of God's preferential earthly means of publicity. Civil society's rapid emergence in our time is perhaps God's most creative work as we enter the third millennium.[13] The future is rich with possibilities for global civil society and God's preferential option for earthly peace. JWT remains a true, effective, and sustainable moral tradition to the extent that we keep it within the richer arc of God's just peacemaking. A Lutheran unified theology of peace serves that end. Finally, because ultimately God gives all earthly peace, prayer is always the encompassing practice of peace.

Every church a peace church: A meditation

Oh, that every church were a peace church. But every church is. It is a theological fact that God calls every church into existence as a peace church. This is what the triune God does through the bonds of the sacrament of baptism. But isn't this calling a terrible thing to waste? And we do waste it, to the world's detriment and to our great shame. Everything that God calls a church to do has the purpose to maximize this call to peace and to minimize its waste. It is no wonder that Luther boldly confessed that God stakes God's own reputation on our baptismal call of peace—both final peace and earthly peace.

What a wonderful confession, "Every church a peace church!" It is also the name of an organized movement to form new peace churches and to transform or convert JWT churches into what the historic peace churches are, pacifist. Now this is perhaps not quite true. I say "perhaps" because there is just enough ambiguity in the movement's vision statement to leave people wondering whether a church must take on the critical side of pacifism (the pure presumption against war) or not. Does "every church a peace church" have a tent designed to embrace JWT churches who support justifiable-war criteria and do so precisely by rededicating themselves to the richer arc of just-peacemaking practices?[14] This is the posture of the ecumenical just-peacemaking movement that we looked at earlier. In this spirit "every church a peace church" is plainly a Christian confession to be acted upon. Then, "every church a peace church"—*Amen!*

Questions for reflection and discussion

1. Are there modern parallels to the "mirror of the prince" documents described above? Do you believe our civic leaders should be "just peacemakers"? How does our government provide—or fail to provide—for the principle of publicity?

2. How have you or groups and communities that you are part of taken on any of the ten practices of just peacemaking? How do you assess the short- and long-term outcomes on the world, in the community and its cultures, and in the lives of individuals? How have these practices affected you emotionally, physically, culturally, and spiritually? How have these practices affected your collaboration and companionship with others? How have collaboration and companionship happened regionally, nationally, and internationally on the institutional level?

3. What does the phrase "every church a peace church" mean to you? How do you see this reflected in your congregation?

4. Can we imagine and anticipate the time when collaborative com-

panionship in just peacemaking becomes a prominent characteristic of Lutheran vocation? How can we extend this collaborative
companionship to "civil society" as well?

7

Four Global Challenges

In this final chapter I introduce four global challenges as we ponder God's preferential future for earthly peace. First, we will look into humanitarian intervention, its problems, and the new turn to "the responsibility to protect." The responsibility to protect sets the stage for our second challenge, the nemesis of global terrorism. Third is the prickly issue of empire and the American future. Finally, we will address the issue of patriotism in a time of war and in an era of global citizenship.

The responsibility to protect

Elie Wiesel, recipient of the Nobel Peace Prize and prophet laureate of the Holocaust, gave a stunning opening address at the dedication of the United States Holocaust Memorial Museum on April 22, 1993. Wiesel ended his address by asking, "What have we learned? We have learned some lessons, minor lessons, perhaps, that we are all responsible, and indifference is a sin and a punishment. And we have learned that when people suffer we cannot remain indifferent." At that moment he turned from the audience, looked vigilantly into the eyes of President Bill Clinton, who sat in the front row of the small auditorium, and said:

> Mr. President, I cannot not tell you something. I have been in the former Yugoslavia last fall. I cannot sleep since for what I have seen. As a Jew I am saying that we must do something to stop the bloodshed in that country! People fight each other and children die. Why? Something, anything must be done.[1]

President Clinton responded by adding a third purpose to the museum's original two purposes, which are (1) to advance and disseminate knowledge of the Holocaust, and (2) to preserve the memory of those who suffered. The new third purpose is to develop moral conscience concerning genocide and crimes against humanity. A year later, however, President Clinton turned his back on Rwanda and the genocidal slaughter of over 800,000 Tutsis and moderate Hutus, not to mention over two million Hutu refugees, by refusing to intervene. He has since called this his biggest failure as president. We the people also failed. Senator Paul Simon, a Lutheran layperson, surmised that if each congressperson had received one hundred letters from constituents urging a U.S. response when the Rwandan crisis first surfaced, our policy would have been different.

The so-called right of humanitarian intervention involves the question of when, if ever, it is appropriate for states to take coercive and in particular military action against another state for the purpose of protecting people at risk in that other state. Humanitarian intervention has been controversial when it has happened, for instance in Kosovo in 1999, and when it has not happened, for instance in Rwanda in 1994 and in Bosnia in 1995.

Four big problems plague the notion of a right to humanitarian intervention. The first is the conflict between the Westphalian and UN principle of nonintervention in the sovereign affairs of another nation, on the one hand, and, on the other, the failure of a sovereign state to protect its citizens from genocide, war crimes, ethnic cleansing, or crimes against humanity or the malevolence of a sovereign state to carry out such atrocities on its own citizens, its resident aliens, or its visitors. Second, the UN has shown itself incapable of undertaking a competent armed intervention when necessary. A third problem concerns the intention that motivates a powerful state to intervene in the affairs of another state even when there is a just cause. In one case, national self-interest motivates a state with the capacity to intervene to do so. In another case, a lack of national self-interest motivates a powerful state to avoid intervention when there is just cause. Fourth is the lack of a moral and political protocol that guides the international community in such circumstances. The right of humanitarian intervention does not include an effective principle of publicity with the safeguards that publicity provides.

In 1999, UN Secretary-General Kofi Annan challenged the 54th General Assembly to resolve the problem. The International Commission on Intervention and State Sovereignty proposed The Responsibility to Protect—R2P as it is called—in December 2001, and the UN's 2005 World Summit agreed to take action on it. R2P's basic theme is that sovereign states have a responsibility to protect those within its borders from avoidable catastrophe, but that when they are unwilling or unable to do so, that responsibility must be borne by the broader community of states. States that fail to protect are often "failed" or failing states.

R2P accomplishes three basic things. First, it clearly recognizes a moral basis inherent in the very concept of sovereignty, which was lacking in the Westphalian notion. At a minimum sovereignty means protecting one's own populations from harm. Failure due to unwillingness or incapacity violates the moral ground of sovereignty. Second, R2P invokes the principle of publicity and implements it as a kind of international republic in these kinds of "conscience-shocking situations crying out for action."[2] Third, R2P identifies three core responsibilities that make up the overarching responsibility to protect: the responsibilities to prevent, to react, and to rebuild. To *prevent* means to address both the root causes and the direct causes that put populations at risk. To *react* means to respond to situations of compelling human need with appropriate measures, which may include coercive measures like sanctions and international prosecution, and in extreme cases military intervention. To *rebuild* applies particularly after a military intervention and means to provide full assistance with recovery, reconstruction, and reconciliation and to address the causes of the harm that the intervention was designed to halt or avert.

All three responsibilities in their ordered relationship capital-ize on Ambrose's maxim, which fills out the natural law of "Do no harm." These responsibilities flow right out of JWT, especially when it is self-consciously placed within the luminous arc of just peace-making. R2P boldly notes that *prevention is the single most important dimension of the responsibility to protect*. Thus two of its core princi-ples are that force protection cannot become the principal objective and that maximum coordination with humanitarian organizations is paramount. When dealing with force protection, R2P specifically cites JWT's criteria of just cause, right intention, legitimate author-ity, last resort, probability of success, and proportionality of means. The end of peace is obvious as is noncombatant immunity, since the lack of civilian immunity is the precipitating event.

The principle of publicity underlies how R2P connects right intention with legitimate authority. Whatever other intentions intervening states may have, the primary intention must be to halt or avert conscience-shocking situations. Therefore, "right intention is better assured with multilateral operations, clearly supported by regional opinion and the victims concerned." Under legitimate authority R2P states, "There is no better or more appropriate body than the United Nations Security Council to authorize military intervention or human protection purposes. The task is not to find alternatives to the Security Council as a source of authority, but to make the Security Council work better than it has." In this spirit it urges the Permanent Five members of the Security Council—China, England, France, Russia, and the United States—to agree not to apply their veto power in matters where their vital state interests are not involved. R2P also recognizes other alternatives if the Security Council tragically fails to protect.

The 2005 World Summit also agreed to take bold action around peacemaking, peacekeeping, and peacebuilding. These three peace actions roughly correspond to R2P's three preventive responsi-bilities. These peace initiatives are designed to preempt and prevent conscience-shocking situations from ever arising. Against these actions there is no law.

Terrorism

"Terrorism haunts our times."[3] 9/11 brought this haunting reality into American homes. Terrorism deliberately and grossly violates the moral obligation of noncombatant immunity. This in itself presents a justifiable cause that calls for public condemnation together with other resolute responses. But what kind will be effective? America responded with "war"—but war is not the only possible response. It is also not the only effective response, though it might be depending on the circumstances.

Because terrorists injure and kill, terrorism looks mostly like a military tactic, only immoral. But terrorism is primarily social and political violence within a larger social and political strategy, policy, and ideology. It is a social and political tactic that targets civilians in order to generate fear and panic in society. It aims to influence people and therefore it is theater and propaganda by means of deadly deeds.

Both state and nonstate actors, sometimes together, use terrorism. We often call these actors "rogue states" and global terrorist networks. Taken together these factors mean that war is only one possible effective response across a range. Some, for instance, have called for "just policing" protocols. The 2005 World Summit agreed to push for a comprehensive convention against terrorism with a strategy that strengthens the international community and weakens terrorist rogue states and global networks. Even though the context of terrorism is different from the context that R2P addresses, R2P provides crucial guidance for a future convention against terrorism, especially about the value of international publicity.

There are other issues that terrorism raises. For instance, perfect security in an imperfect world is not possible. How do we negotiate then the tradeoff between heightened security and weaker civil and political rights? What kind of security is too much because it weakens our rights, which make a free life possible? What kind of security is too little because it leaves us a free life too vulnerable to violence and death? How do we live with a certain level of "healthy fear," on the one hand, and yet live a "healthy life" beyond fear on the other hand? Since religious categories have emerged along with the current intensification of global terrorism, how can we contribute to interfaith understanding and to collaboration for earthly peace?

American empire?

In his 2004 State of the Union Address, President Bush said: "America is a nation with a mission, and that mission comes from our most basic beliefs. We have no desire to dominate, no ambitions of empire."[4] But why does the president have to offer this assurance to the nation and the world?

Four days after the president's 2004 address Vice President Dick Cheney, in Davos, Switzerland, again disavowed any ambitions to empire and used a territorial definition of empire. The president had first stated this kind of disavowal in his West Point graduation speech on June 1, 2002, four quotations from which show up as official epigrams in *The National Security Strategy of the United States of America*, which officially houses much of what has become known as the "Bush Doctrine." The President denied empire again in similar terms on November 11, 2002, in a speech at a White House reception for veterans, saying, "We have no territorial ambitions, we don't seek an empire."[5] Like the vice president, the president uses a territorial definition when he denies that America is, or aspires to be, an empire.

When real estate was the prime way to expand a nation's economic wealth and political power, the definition of empire was attached to territory. Now, however, access to economic resources and markets and to sources of cultural capital is the path to wealth, power, and prestige. Therefore, establishing and expanding an empire now comes by gaining and dominating access to economic markets and seedbeds of culture. In different times of world history, there have been other models of empire. For instance, in some eras controlling religion has been the key. The neoconservative movement, which has influenced Mr. Bush's administration, desires an ever-expanding unipolar world, marked by growing American primacy and full-spectrum dominance.[6]

Already in the late 1950s, America's most famous twentieth-century theologian, Reinhold Niebuhr, described an America "so desperately anxious not to be an empire." In the twenty-first century prominent Americans have advocated a kinder, gentler "empire lite," or urged America to "be imperial without being imperialist." Some assert that empire is our national "default" destiny. George Washington warned the young nation about foreign adventurism and ever since the ambition of empire has been our permanent temptation. Succumbing to this temptation remains a failed patriotism.

The patriotism of empire comes from the otherwise legitimate desire to live securely. A brief history of the failed patriotism of empire began already with the British invasion that started the War of 1812. President James Monroe assigned his secretary of state, John Quincy Adams, the task of developing the "Monroe Doctrine." Adams's principle was to achieve security through expansion. In 1811 he had already written to his mother, Abigail, that America was "destined by God and nature" to expand. A few years later he noted, "any effort on our part to reason the world out of a belief that we are ambitious will have no other effect than to convince them that we add to our ambition hypocrisy."[7]

Adams carried out the Monroe Doctrine's expansionist principle of empire around three foreign policy practices: unilateral visioning, waging a blur of preemptive-preventive wars, and pursuing a preponderance of American power rather than a balance among several powers. President Andrew Jackson executed the Monroe Doctrine by waging an intentionally blurred combination of preemptive and preventive wars that dispossessed Native Americans of their lands and self-determination. Presidents James Polk, William McKinley, Theodore Roosevelt, William Taft, and, early in his administration, Woodrow Wilson, all carried out empire to varying degrees and with differing skill.

John Gaddis notes that President Bush "whether intentionally or not, has been drawing upon a set of traditions that go back" to the Monroe Doctrine. The Bush Doctrine only "reflects a return to an old position, not the emergence of a new one." This is what the *National Security Strategy* does when it permissively blurs preemption and prevention, stresses "our best defense is a good offense," and pursues "regime change." Like Gaddis, many think that Adams's three expansionist practices of empire are and should remain America's "default: when in doubt, fall back on these." Soon after 9/11 a stunned President defaulted and has had "no doubt" since.[8]

President Bush has continued, in his words, to "stay the course."[9] In his second inaugural address of January 20, 2005, he asserted, "We are led, by events and common sense, to one conclusion: The survival of liberty in our land increasingly depends on the success of liberty in other lands. The best hope for peace in our world is the expansion of freedom in all the world." On January 10, 2007, Mr. Bush again used familiar rhetoric, "the advance of freedom is the calling of our time," and credited our national calling to "the Author of Liberty."[10] On the surface the words can sound noble. But as the old saying goes, the devil is in the details, and here trouble lies in words like *expand* and *advance*. The policy and strategy tsunami that powers this rhetoric is Adams's old unilateralism combined with the permissive blurring of preemptive-preventive war.

Patriotism, repentance, and civic international publicity

While the expansionist empire of Adams, Polk, McKinley, and others is one American tradition, most Americans, precisely on a common-sense level of American patriotism, relate to a richer set of traditions embodied in the likes of Washington, Jefferson, Lincoln, and Franklin Delano Roosevelt. In fact, what exploded at Pearl Harbor on December 7, 1941, as a national security crisis became, ironically, a hopeful opportunity for FDR. He repelled the tradition and practices of an expansionist American empire as failed patriotism. Instead, he led America in a more civic international-ist direction. Those who followed him helped build the United Nations, the jurisprudence of International Humanitarian Law, and the traditions of international publicity with its preference for just peacemaking.

Before finishing, let us retrieve Luther's understanding that all wars, especially those waged justifiably, are to be repentant wars. As we saw earlier, this was his posture for waging war against the Turk. On October 31, 1517, Luther had already engraved repentance into the very first thesis of his famous ninety-five: "When our Lord and Master Jesus Christ said, 'Repent,' he willed the entire life of believ-ers to be one of repentance." Even when Christians are only a few, they should set the pace for national repentance in a just war.

In American history President Abraham Lincoln picked up on the same biblical pervasiveness of repentance in the face of war. Already as a U.S. congressman, Lincoln implored "good citizens and patriots" to undergo "genuine repentance" and "to confess their [political] sins and transgressions" as a national practice of truth. This was January 12, 1848, twenty months after President James Polk had declared war on Mexico. Shortly after President Lincoln issued the Emancipation Proclamation on January 1, 1863, and eight months before his Gettysburg Address in November 1863 he issued a "Proclamation Appointing a National Fast Day": "And whereas it is the duty of nations as well as of men, to own their dependence upon the overruling power of God, to confess their sins and trans-gressions, in humble sorrow, yet with assured hope that genuine repentance will lead to mercy and pardon . . ." Only by walking the path through national repentance could America begin "to bind up the nation's wounds;" "to do all which may achieve and cherish a just, and lasting peace, among ourselves, and with all nations;" and to do so "with malice toward none; with charity for all."[11]

Against repentant patriotism there is no law! Indeed, repentant patriotism binds JWT to the rich arc of just peacemaking, God's preferential future for earthly peace.

Questions for reflection and discussion

1. When do you think humanitarian intervention in another sovereign nation is appropriate? Why? What role should national self-interest play in determining whether to intervene? What role should the UN play?

2. When it comes to dealing with threats of terrorism, how do you feel we should balance concerns about security with concerns about civil liberties? Is racial or ethnic profiling ever an appropriate security response? Why or why not?

3. If one defines "empire" in terms of economic, cultural, and market power and influence, do you believe it is right to consider the United States as an empire? How do our recent military endeavors, particularly in the Middle East, contribute to the perception of American empire?

4. What do you think "repentant patriotism" looks like? On a national basis? On a community basis? On an individual basis?

Notes

All Web sites were accessed and live as of June 1, 2007.

Introduction

1. *Meet the Press with Tim Russert*, NBC News, "Interview with President George W. Bush," Feb. 13, 2004; www.msnbc.msn.com/id/4179618/.

2. See "President's Remarks at National Day of Prayer and Remembrance," September 14, 2001; www.whitehouse.gov/news/releases/2001/09/20010914-2.html. This quotation became one of the official epigrams of "The National Security Strategy of the United States of America" (September 2002); www.whitehouse.gov/nsc/nssintro.html.

3. www.whitehouse.gov/news/releases/2003/03/20030322.html

4. James Turner Johnson, *Just War Tradition and the Restraint of War* (Princeton: Princeton University Press, 1981), xxi.

5. A Lutheran theology of peace begins with a clear distinction between God's final peace and God's earthly peace, based on the biblical distinction between law and gospel. Making this distinction assures the proper relationship of God's final and earthly peace. See the ELCA social statement *For Peace in God's World* (1995); www.elca.org/socialstatements/peace/.

Chapter 1

1. See *Exsurge Domine*; www.papalencyclicals.net/Leo10/l10exdom.htm.

2. Martin Luther, "Defense and Explanation of All the Articles," *Luther's Works* 32:89–90. (American Edition of *Luther's Works*, St. Louis and Philadelphia, 1955-1986) (hereafter *LW*)

3. *The Augsburg Confession* in *The Book of Concord: The Confessions of the Evangelical Lutheran Church*, eds. Robert Kolb and Timothy J. Wengert (Minneapolis: Fortress Press, 2000), 49–50.

4. *The Large Catechism* in Kolb and Wengert, eds., *The Book of Concord*, 389.

Chapter 2

1. Michael Walzer, *Just and Unjust Wars: A Moral Argument with Historical Illustrations*, 3rd ed. (New York: Basic Books, 2000), 21.

2. Martin L. Cook, *The Moral Warrior: Ethics and Service in the U.S. Military* (Albany: State University of New York Press, 2004), 32.

Chapter 3

1. Cicero, *On Duties*, 1.4, 11-13; www.constitution.org/rom/de_officiis .htm.

2. Ambrose, *On the Duties of the Clergy*, 1.28; 1.27; 1.36; www.newadvent.org/fathers/34011.htm (accessed June 1, 2007). He borrowed this insight from Cicero's analysis of passive and active justice and injustice (*On Duties*, 1.7, 9). Passive (negative) justice is to do no harm; active (positive) justice is to do good. Active injustice is to do harm to another; passive injustice is to neglect to do good to another when you can.

3. Ambrose, *On the Duties of the Clergy*, 1.27; Ambrose, *Discourse on Luke's Gospel*, 5.73, quoted in Louis J. Swift, *The Early Fathers on War and Military Service* (Wilmington: Glazier, 1983), 100; Ambrose, *Discourse on Psalm 118*, 15.22, quoted in Swift, *The Early Fathers on War and Military Service*, 103.

4. Augustine, *Letter 189 (A.D. 418)* to Count Boniface, 6; www.newadvent.org/fathers/1102189.htm.

5. Augustine, *City of God*, 19.7; www.newadvent.org/fathers/1201.htm. For "right intention" in the subjective sense and for "legitimate authority" see Augustine, *Reply to Faustus the Manichaean (Contra Faustum)*, 22.74-75; www.newadvent.org/fathers/140622.htm.

6. Augustine, *City of God*, 19.27.

7. See James Turner Johnson, *The Quest for Peace* (Princeton: Princeton University Press, 1987), 9–16; for the standard account see Roland Bainton, *Christian Attitudes toward War and Peace* (New York: Abingdon Press, 1960).

8. Augustine, *Letter 47 (A.D. 398),* to Publicola, 5; www.newadvent.org/fathers/1102047.htm.

9. Augustine, *Letter 138 (A.D. 412),* to Marcellinus, 2.14; www.newadvent.org/fathers/1102138.htm. Also see Augustine's exploration of "preparation of heart" in *On the Sermon on the Mount*, 1.19 at www.newadvent.org/fathers/16011.htm.

10. Augustine, *Letter 185,* to Boniface, 19; 20; 21; 21; www.newadvent.org/fathers/1102185.htm.

11. Thomas Aquinas, *Summa Theologicus*, 2-2.40.1; www.newadvent. org/summa/3040.htm.

12. Aquinas, *Summa Theologicus*, 2-2.188.3.

Chapter 4

1. Martin Luther, *Whether Soldiers Too Can Be Saved* in *Luther's Works*, American Edition, 55 vols. (Philadelphia: Fortress Press; St. Louis: Concordia Publishing House, 1955–1986), 46:121 (hereafter *LW*).

2. Martin Luther, *Temporal Authority: To What Extent It Should Be Obeyed*, in *LW* 45:88.

3. Ibid., 45:91–92.

4. Ibid., 45:94.

5. Ibid.

6. Luther, *Whether Soldiers Too Can Be Saved*, *LW* 46:96.

7. Luther, *Temporal Authority*, *LW* 46:105, 106 (2x), 107, 108 (2x).

8. In support he cited Paul (Rom. 13:3, 7), Peter (1 Peter 2:13), Jesus (Matt. 22:21), David (Ps. 115:16), Moses (Gen. 1:26), and again Peter (Acts 5:29). Ibid., 45:114, 110–11.

9. See Martin Luther, *Commentary on Psalm 82*, *LW* 13:6167; *On the Jews and Their Lies*, *LW* 47:262–74.

10. Luther, *On War against the Turk*, in *LW* 46:65, 186.

11. Ibid., 46:185, 171; also 46:170.

12. Luther, *Treatise on Good Works*, *LW* 44:100.

13. Francisco de Vitoria, *On the Indians*, 1.4-24, 2.1-2; and Vitoria, *On the Law of War*, 11-13; www.constitution.org/victoria/victoria.txt. Cicero's *On Duties* was the second book to be printed on the Gutenberg press, second after the Bible. This testifies to its status from the 15th century on.

14. Vitoria, *On the Indians*, 2.7-15; 10.

15. Ibid., 3.11-13.

16. Vitoria, *On the Law of War*, 20-24.

17. Ibid., 34-60.

18. Hugo Grotius, *On the Law of War and Peace*, Prolegomena.28; www.lonang.com/exlibris/grotius/index.html.

19. See *Treaty of Westphalia* (October 24, 1648) at www.yale.edu/law-web/avalon/westphal.htm.

20. Grotius, *On the Law of War and Peace*, 1.1.1-4; also see 1.1.10-14.

21. Ibid., Prolegomena.11; also 1.1.10.

22. Ibid., 2.1.1-4; also see 2.20.1-40.

23. Ibid., 1.3.7

24. Ibid., 2.26.4; also see 2.22.4-17; 2.23.1-9; 3.3.1-14.

25. Ibid., 2.20.43; 2.1.5; 2.1.17; 2.20.41; on proportionality, see 2.24.5-7.

26. Ibid., 2.26.3.

27. Ibid., 3.11.7; 3.1.4; 3.1.6-20; 3.20.1-60.

28. Ibid., 3.11.8.

29. Ibid., 3.25.1; on good faith in general, see 3.19-25.

30. For the Red Cross movement and the 1864 Geneva Convention see www.icrc.org/web/eng/siteeng0.nsf/html/57JNVP; for the Lieber Code see www.icrc.org/ihl.nsf/INTRO/110?OpenDocument or www.yale.edu/lawweb/avalon/lieber.htm.

31. See The Hague Conventions, as well as a comprehensive list of treaties and documents comprising IHL at www.icrc.org/ihl.nsf or www.yale.edu/lawweb/avalon/lawofwar/lawwar.htm..

32. See the *United Nations Charter* at www.un.org/aboutun/charter/.

33. Principle VI of *Principles of International Law Recognized in the Charter of the Nüremberg Tribunal and in the Judgment of the Tribunal, 1950* sets out and defines three kinds of crime that violate IHL: crimes against peace, war crimes, and crimes against humanity; see www.icrc.org/ihl.nsf/FULL/390?OpenDocument.

34. See the Geneva Conventions I-IV and Protocols I-III; www.icrc.org/Web/Eng/siteeng0.nsf/html/genevaconventions.

Chapter 5

1. National Conference of Catholic Bishops, *The Challenge of Peace: God's Promise and Our Response*, paragraph 1; www.osjspm.org/the_challenge_of_peace_1.aspx.

2. Their "Summary" appears at the front of the printed version of *The Challenge of Peace* but not in the online version.

3. National Conference of Catholic Bishops, *The Harvest of Justice Is Sown in Peace: A Reflection on the Tenth Anniversary of The Challenge of Peace*, I.B; www.nccbuscc.org/sdwp/harvest.htm.

4. Pope John XXIII, *Pacem in Terris* (April 11, 1963), §§109–11; www.vatican.va/holy_father/john_xxiii/encyclicals/documents/hf_j-xxiii_enc_11041963_pacem_en.html; and *Gaudium et Spes,* or *Pastoral Constitution on the Church in the Modern World*, 81; www.vatican.va/archive/hist_councils/ii_vatican_council/documents/vat-ii_cons_19651207_gaudium-et-spes_en.html.

5. *Pacem in Terris*, 113, 127; *Pastoral Constitution*, 80.

6. *The Challenge of Peace*, 7, 120, 126, 68; *Pastoral Constitution*, 78.

7. *Pastoral Constitution*, 4; *The Challenge of Peace*, 242.

8. Pope Paul VI, *Address to the General Assembly of the United Nations* (1965), 2, as cited in *The Challenge of Peace*, 267.

9. *Pacem in Terris*, 161–62.

Chapter 6

1. Martin Luther, *The Large Catechism*, in *The Confessions of the Evangelical Lutheran Church*, eds. Robert Kolb and Timothy J. Wengert (Minneapolis: Fortress Press, 2000), 352.

2. Luther, *Commentary on Psalm 82*, in *LW* 13:45.

3. Ibid., *LW* 13:46–47.

4. Ibid., *LW* 13:53.

5. Ibid., *LW* 13:53–54.

6. Luther, *Commentary on Psalm 82*, *LW* 13:55, 56. For Luther on the scepter also see *Commentary on Psalm 45*, in *LW* 12:236–47.

7. Luther, *Commentary on Psalm 82*, *LW* 13:49.

8. Ibid., *LW* 13:49–50.

9. Luther, *Commentary on Psalm 101*, in *LW* 13:157, 154, 160, 157, 155.

10. Glen Stassen, ed., *Just Peacemaking: Ten Practices for Abolishing War* (Cleveland: Pilgrim Press, 1998).

11. Already in 1982 the American Lutheran Church used the term *peacemaking* in its social statement, *Mandate for Peacemaking* (Minneapolis: Augsburg, 1982); Lutherans have generally used *peacemaking* at least since that time.

12. For more information on LSA, go to www.lutheranservices.org.

13. For a fuller exploration of civil society and the God question see Gary M. Simpson, et al., *Our Callings in the Community* (St. Paul: Centered Life, 2006).

14. See Every Church A Peace Church's vision statement in the context of its "short history" statement at ecapc.org/.

Chapter 7

1. Elie Wiesel, "Remarks at the Dedication Ceremonies for the United States Holocaust Memorial Museum, April 22, 1993"; www.ushmm.org/research/library/faq/06/01/ceremony/index.php?content=wiesel

2. See the "Synopsis" in The International Commission of Intervention and State Sovereignty, *The Responsibility to Protect* (December 2001); www.iciss.ca/report-en.asp. Also see United Nations, *2005 World Summit Outcome: Fact Sheet*, High Level Plenary Meeting, 14–16 September 2005; www.un.org/summit2005/presskit/fact_sheet.pdf (accessed June 4, 2007). What follows comes right from the International Commission of Intervention and State Sovereignty document in light of what we have learned in our review of JWT and just peacemaking.

3. Evangelical Lutheran Church in America, *Living in a Time of Terrorism* (2004); www.elca.org/socialstatements/terrorism/. This is a helpful initial approach.

4. President George W. Bush, *State of the Union Address* (2004); www.whitehouse.gov/news/releases/2004/01/print20040120-7.html.

5. Vice President Dick Cheney in Davos, Switzerland, at www.whitehouse.gov/news/releases/2004/01/print/20040124-1.html; President George W. Bush at West Point graduation, at www.whitehouse.gov/news/releases/2002/06/20020601-3.html; *The National Security Strategy of the United States of America* (hereafter *NSS*) at www.whitehouse.gov/nsc/nss.html; President George W. Bush at the White House at www.whitehouse.gov/news/releases/2002/11/print/20021111-2.html.

6. For prominent neoconservative thinking, see *Present Dangers: Crisis and Opportunity in American Foreign and Defense Policy*, ed. Robert Kagan and William Kristol (San Francisco: Encounter, 2000); also see *Statement of Principles* (June 3, 1997), Project for the New American Century at www.newamericancentury.org/); also see Thomas Donnelly, "Brave New World: An Enduring *Pax Americana*," *National Security Outlook*, American Enterprise Institute, April 1, 2003, at www.aei.org/publications/pubID.16710/pub_detail.asp.

7. John Gaddis, *Surprise, Security, and the American Experience* (Cambridge: Harvard University Press, 2004), 26–27. Gaddis is a prominent political and military Yale University historian.

8. Ibid., 31,16, 31. The neoconservative thinkers had been advocating this unipolar, empire default since the 1989 collapse of the Soviet Union.

9. A good example is the president's February 8, 2004, interview on NBC's *Meet the Press* with Tim Russert at www.msnbc.msn.com/id/4179618/.

10. President George W. Bush, "Second Inaugural Address" (January 20,2005),at www.whitehouse.gov/news/releases/2005/01/print/20050120-

1.html; see President George W. Bush, "President's Address to the Nation," (January 10, 2007) at www.whitehouse.gov/news/releases/2007/01/20070110-7.html.

11. Abraham Lincoln, "Speech in United States House of Representatives: The War with Mexico," in *Collected Works*, vol. 1 (New Brunswick, N.J.: Rutgers University Press, 1953–1955), 432, 433, 431; Abraham Lincoln, "Proclamation Appointing a National Fast Day," in *Collected Works*, 6:155; President Lincoln's memorable Second Inaugural Address of March 4, 1865, less than six weeks before he was assassinated; see www.ourdocuments.gov/doc.php?doc=38&page=transcript.

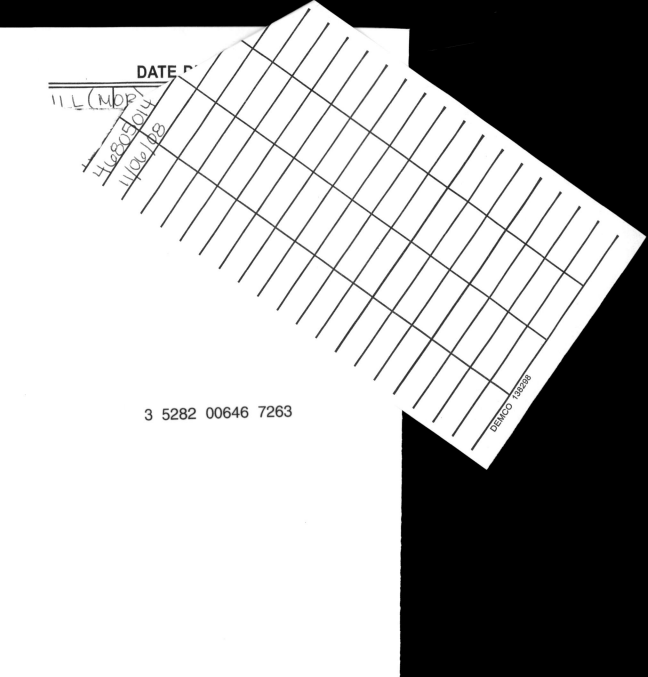

3 5282 00646 7263

For Further Reading

All Web sites were accessed and live as of June 1, 2007.

Cahill, Lisa Sowle. *Love Your Enemies: Discipleship, Pacifism, and Just War Theory*. Minneapolis: Fortress Press, 1994.

Evangelical Lutheran Church in America. *For Peace in God's World*. Chicago: ELCA, 1995. www.elca.org/socialstatements/peace/.

Johnson, James Turner. *Just War Tradition and the Restraint of War*. Princeton: Princeton University Press, 1981.

Maguire, Daniel C. *The Horrors We Bless: Rethinking the Just War Legacy*, Facets Books. Minneapolis: Fortress Press, 2007.

National Conference of Catholic Bishops. *The Challenge of Peace: God's Promise and Our Response*. Washington, D.C.: United States Catholic Conference, 1983. www.osjspm.org/the_challenge_of_peace_1.aspx.

———. *The Harvest of Justice Is Sown in Peace: A Reflection on the Tenth Anniversary of The Challenge of Peace*, I.B. Washington, D.C.: United States Catholic Conference, 1994. www.nccbuscc.org/sdwp/harvest.htm.

Pope John XXIII. *Pacem in Terris*. April 11, 1963. §§109–11. www.vatican.va/holy_father/john_xxiii/encyclicals/documents/hf_j-xxiii_enc_11041963_pacem_en.html.

Simpson, Gary M., et al., *Our Callings in the Community*. St. Paul: Centered Life, 2006.

Stassen, Glen, ed., *Just Peacemaking: Ten Practices for Abolishing War*. Cleveland: Pilgrim Press, 1998.

Walzer, Michael. *Just and Unjust Wars: A Moral Argument with Historical Illustrations*. 3rd ed. New York: Basic Books, 2000.